Your Family's Guide To A Secure Future

COPYRIGHT © 2014 Ian King, CFPCM
ALL RIGHTS RESERVED

Published by Ian King Financial Planning Ltd.

Your Family's Guide To A Secure Future

COPYRIGHT © 2014 Ian King, CFP^{CM}
Professional & Chartered Financial Planner

ALL RIGHTS RESERVED

thefamilylegacysolution.co.uk

The Family Legacy Solution™ is a trading style of Ian King Financial Planning Ltd, which is authorised and regulated by the Financial Conduct Authority (Firm Reference Number: 630542). Registered in England and Wales: 08469955.

Published by Ian King Financial Planning Ltd.
The Old Vicarage, Market Street, Castle Donington, Derbyshire DE74 2JB

NO PART OF THIS BOOK MAY BE REPRODUCED OR TRANSMITTED IN ANY FORM OR ANY MANNER, ELECTRONIC OR MECHANICAL, INCLUDING PHOTOCOPYING, RECORDING OR BY ANY INFORMATION STORAGE AND RETRIEVAL SYSTEM, WITHOUT PERMISSION IN WRITING FROM THE AUTHOR.

ISBN: 978-0-9931731-0-3

INTRODUCTION 1
- This Book Is for You 2
- A Chapter-by-Chapter Preview 4

1. GETTING PROFESSIONAL HELP 7
- Historically, Financial Services Was Product-Oriented 8
- Beware Potential Conflicts of Interest 9
- The Value of Financial Planning 11
- Choosing the Right Financial Planner 14
- Do-it-yourself Tasks versus Tasks Best Left to Planners . 16

2. EXPLORING YOUR CAPABILITIES 19
- Involve Your Spouse/Partner in the Process 20
- Budget Planning 22
- Budgeting Your Time 25
- The Consequences of Not Creating a Budget 27
- Avoid These Common Mistakes 29
- Spendthrifts and Hoarders 31
- 2A: The Capability Explorer 34
- 2B: The Budget Extender 35

3. BREATHING LIFE INTO VISIONS AND GOALS 37
- Set Your Sights High! 38
- Common Mistakes in Goal-Setting 39
- Identifying Opportunities, Threats and Resources 42
- Record Your Goals 44
- 3A. Identifying Opportunities, Threats and Resources 47

4. FAMILY IMPACT DISCUSSIONS 49
- Funding Higher Education 52
- Long-Term Care 53
- Some Basics Facts about Wills 56
- Transferring Values, Knowledge and Experience 59
- Charitable Giving 60
- Lifetime Gifts 61

5. IMPLEMENTING YOUR FINANCIAL PLAN 67
- Common Obstacles to Implementation 68
- A Structured Process 71

6. CHOOSING AN INVESTMENT STRATEGY 73
- Saving versus Investing 73

What Is Investment Risk? 74
Assessing Your Risk Tolerance 76
The Importance of Strategic Asset Allocation 80
Tactical Asset Allocation Decisions 81
K.I.S.S. 82
Matching Assets to Objectives 84
Diversification: The "Free Lunch" of Investing 85
Be Wary of Guarantees 87
The Need for Transparency 88
Don't Underestimate the Need for Liquidity 90
Passive vs. Active Management 91
Costs 92
When to Review Investment Performance 93
Avoid Speculation 94
Contrarianism 95
Prepare for Disappointment 97
Exploit Time, Not Timing 97
Rebalancing 98
Don't Let the "Tax Tail" Wag the "Investment Dog" 99
Create a Written Investment Policy Mandate 100
The Voice of Reason 102
6A. Clarity Developer 104
Understanding Your Philosophy Towards Investments 105

7. PROGRESS APPRAISALS 109
The Door Should Always Be Open 109
Focus on Ends, Not Just Means 110

APPENDIX 113
Budget Planning 113
The Six Jars Philosophy 114
Insurance 115
Wills and Lasting Power of Attorney 116

Dedication

To Mum and Dad. Thank you.

Acknowledgments

The success that I have had to date and indeed this book couldn't have happened without the help and dedication of many people including the following:

My family and friends, particularly my mother Beryl, father Graham, and sister Jennifer.

The members of my work team, both past and present.

The team and members at the Institute of Financial Planning (IFP).

The team and participants at the Strategic Coach® program.

For his assistance in helping me put together this book, Peter Gerardo.

Finally, but by no means least, the support, insight and encouragement offered to me by my long-standing clients.

About the Author

Seizing his passion for helping clients and their families achieve a brighter and more rewarding future, Ian is the founder and inspiration behind The Family Legacy Solution™ and Ian King Financial Planning Ltd. With over ten years of experience in advising clients, Ian is able to call upon a wealth of knowledge and experience in developing and delivering a wide range of client solutions. These solutions range from legacy and estate planning, retirement planning to long-term care planning.

Always seeking to improve both the service to his clients and his own professional development, Ian is proud to be a Fellow of the Personal Finance Society and a Chartered Financial Planner. He has also achieved the status of Certified Financial PlannerCM.

In order to help develop his skills further and give a much stronger service to his clients he also enjoys spending time with his team to help put processes in place and develop their skills and knowledge of the financial services industry.

Away from the office Ian's interests include travelling to new and wonderful places, language learning, trips to the movies and spending time with friends and family.

Introduction

THIS BOOK IS FOR READERS WHO WISH TO build a brighter future for themselves and the people they care about. Please note, however, that this is not an investment planning or retirement planning "how-to" guide. It is an overview of the issues you'll need to address, in tandem with a good Financial Planner, to ensure that a bright and financially secure future becomes your reality and not just a wistful daydream. Just as important, The Family Legacy Solution™ also focuses on the transfer of financial resources to beneficiaries such as spouses, children, grandchildren, and charitable causes, as well as transferring your values, time, and wisdom – during and after your lifetime.

As a Chartered Financial Planner and Certified Financial Planner, I'm often tasked with helping people leave a financial legacy to others. Although the work involves a lot of "number-crunching," what fascinates me is the impact these legacies can – and do – have on the beneficiaries and the people around them, including the community. When a legacy plan is effectively implemented, funds are delivered to the next generation in a quick, efficient manner. In my view, however, a Financial Planner's role should not be limited to achieving only financial goals. It must encompass more than just money.

In many ways the values, experiences, and wisdom bequeathed to future generations can be more important than the impact of one's financial legacy. For example, a child's outlook toward relationships, their environment, money, work, and a host of other things is closely tied to the values and lessons handed down from parents. Often, these values make such a lasting imprint upon us that they can fix our attitudes and behaviours for decades or even for life.

I think the adage "clogs to clogs in three generations" perfectly encapsulates the importance of transferring your time, energy, and values within any legacy. The wealth derived from a successful parent in the first generation can easily be passed to the next, but intangible assets – the values, memories, and time spent with the younger generations – are too often lost to the grave. If these core values erode in the decades that follow, so does the financial legacy.

When discussing the legacies my clients would like to leave, I often ask what the long-term impact would be upon their beneficiaries if they (and/or their spouses/partners) had died yesterday. If they took all of their property, cash, pensions, businesses, investments, and life policy proceeds and dumped them onto their children, how would the beneficiaries' lives change? Would these changes be positive or would they become a burden?

How would you answer this question?

Many of my clients are concerned about the impact such windfalls will have on their children's attitude toward money, work, and material possessions, and how their personal relationships might be affected by such life-changing sums. Remember, a meaningful financial legacy doesn't need to be in the multi-millions; a bequest of just a few thousand pounds can have a profound effect on one's attitudes and behaviours.

One of my key motivations in establishing The Family Legacy Solution, therefore, was to create the maximum positive impact from the legacies left within families and to minimise any negative consequences. By reading this book and working closely with the right Financial Planner, you'll be better prepared to leave the kind of legacy that your loved ones deserve whilst fulfilling your own dreams and ambitions – dreams and ambitions that might have seemed impossible (or even ludicrous) before you embarked upon the legacy planning process.

This Book Is for You ...

... If you're willing to be proactive to build that brighter future for yourself and your loved ones. Although a good Financial Planner will act as a leader and consultant regarding your personal and financial goals, and will present the best options to achieve them, the planner cannot do it alone. At a minimum, you must be willing to ask, and be asked, some difficult questions and also be willing to (possibly) make changes to your attitudes, habits, and lifestyle. (You must also understand, of course, that a Financial Planner's expertise comes with certain fees.)

Whilst everyone could benefit from the principles outlined in this book, it is most suited for people who are (1) close to retirement or who are already retired; and (2) mostly free of debt, with surplus financial resources (or potential resources) at their disposal – though the resources needn't be vast. You don't need x amount of assets or y amount of income to qualify for legacy planning. Finally, from a technical standpoint, you'll receive the most benefit from this book if you reside and are domiciled in the U.K., especially England or Wales.

This book is *not* for you if you are uninterested in being proactive. If you like to "go with the flow" or if you genuinely believe that things can't get any better, you'll be wasting your time. On the other hand, if you're merely sceptical about the benefits of financial and legacy planning – if you're just not convinced it's possible to fulfill your vision for the future, give me the chance to convince you otherwise.

I've worked with many sceptics over the years. Some thought they couldn't afford financial planning or saw no value in it. Others believed they could never afford to stop working, so why bother planning for post-retirement? Time and again, I've proven sceptics wrong, though it took some time and convincing. But ultimately, the results spoke for themselves.

I recently met with a couple who were totally disorganised in terms of their finances and personal goals, and our first discussion wasn't going well. I was trying to learn a bit more about them by asking questions like, "What are your household expenditures? What do you do with your time? Tell me about some of the policies, pensions, and other assets you own." They responded by hunting for various odds-and-sods around the house, pulling files from here and digging up statements there. While they were pursuing this archaeological quest, my eyes wandered about the home – a relatively modest house that clearly hadn't seen much upkeep in recent years. In fact, it was pretty messy.

I thought, "This isn't going to go anywhere. The husband has a reasonably sized pension scheme, but they're not giving me anything that resembles 'positive feedback.' I can see this from their body language. They don't know what they want or what to do, and I'm not sure they care."

I decided to change my approach. "When would you like to retire?" I asked.

"*Now*," they replied.

The husband was in his early sixties, and the wife in her late fifties, so I said, "Okay, what would it mean if you could retire now? And why would you want to retire now?"

I couldn't get a word in edgeways for 15 minutes, as they talked about how much they hated their jobs, and how much they wanted to pursue this activity or that goal. The dynamic completely changed. Still, even after examining the bits and pieces of paper they'd rummaged, including some good state pension entitlements that were coming in five or ten years, they believed they couldn't retire.

I said, "If I could put together a plan for you – if I could demonstrate that you *could* retire tomorrow – would that be of interest to you?"

"Of course! But we don't think we'll be able to do it."

"It's pay-to-see," I said. "Here's the fee for finding out. Interested?"

They agreed, and after spending a little time exchanging more information, I got back to them and said, "Congratulations. You *can* retire tomorrow."

And they have.

I went to see them a few months ago for our annual review. They haven't quite accomplished everything they wanted to do, but their lives are a lot better than before. *A lot better.*

Your life can also be a lot better, too. "Progress, not perfection" is a wise mantra. All it takes is an open mind, a willingness to dream (and dream big), and a commitment to putting in the time and effort needed to implement the six steps described in Chapters 2 through 7.

A Chapter-by-Chapter Preview

In **Chapter 1: Getting Professional Help**, I discuss the mission of Financial Planners and offer some background on the financial services industry in the U.K. I also address key differences between the fee structures and services of Financial Planners and financial advisers, and offer guidelines on screening planners to determine whether they are a good fit for you.

Chapter 2: Exploring Your Capabilities represents the first phase of The Family Legacy Solution six-step planning process. Legacy planning begins with an assessment of your financial resources and commitments, along with what's coming in and going out. This chapter outlines how to approach the process. Topics include core versus discretionary spending; projecting how investments and other assets will perform in the years ahead; how your Financial Planner can help you value and understand your pension benefits and options; and preparing a realistic budget.

Chapter 3: Breathing Life into Your Visions and Goals addresses the financial and non-financial impacts that financial planning can have on you, your family, and your community. Here I focus on why legacy planning involves more than identifying suitable investment products, but also requires that you develop a vision and strategy. I'll discuss the biggest mistakes made during this phase, as well as our approach to identifying opportunities, threats, and resources. In addition, I'll focus on how to develop and maintain clarity throughout the process and explain how legacy planning can build a better lifestyle *today*, as well as after retirement.

Chapter 4: Family Impact Discussions offers guidance on when, where, and how to disseminate your financial plan to the entire family, making your beneficiaries aware of not just what they will receive, but also of any responsibilities they will face. The chapter also covers the basics of funding a higher education for your children and grandchildren; funding long-term nursing care in the face of rising costs; the fundamentals of Wills and estate planning; and best practices for transferring your values, knowledge, and experiences to the next generation. In addition, I'll outline how you can exercise more control over the time and money you donate to charitable causes, and will also discuss the benefits of "lifetime giving."

Chapter 5: Choosing an Investment Strategy is for those of you who need a comprehensive investment strategy – not everyone does. Here, I discuss how a Financial Planner can assess your risk tolerance and evaluate various "what if" scenarios that might affect your expenditures and the health of your portfolio, e.g. inflation, death, illness, or injury.

I'll also talk about building portfolios to meet your short-term, medium-term, and long-term needs, discuss the benefits of diversification, and focus on the virtues of simplicity, transparency, and maintaining a level head in turbulent markets.

Chapter 6: Implementing Your Financial Plan is where thoughts are translated into action. Now that you've created a detailed vision and a realistic budget, shared your plans with the family, and chosen a wise investment strategy, it's time to put the plan into action. I'll explain common roadblocks to effectively implementing your plan and how a good Financial Planner can help you overcome them. I'll also outline some effective methods of minimising your tax burden.

In *Chapter 7: Progress Appraisals*, I focus on when, why, and how you and your planner should review the plan, as well as circumstances that might warrant adjustments to your strategy.

As a bonus, I've included information and insights on budget planning, saving, insurance, and Wills for members of the younger generation. This material can be found in the *Appendix*, which you should share with your children and grandchildren.

There's never a "wrong" time to start developing a legacy or financial plan. The longer you wait, the harder it can be to change ingrained attitudes and habits. The sooner you start, the sooner you and your family will enjoy the kind of future you've always wanted.

1. Getting Professional Help

GIVEN THE PERILS OF NAVIGATING the complex and confusing universe of financial products – not to mention turbulent financial markets – you would think most people would avail themselves of the services of an expert, someone skilled in managing savings and investments, someone who routinely prevents clients from succumbing to ignorance, irrational exuberance, or blind panic as he guides them toward the financial "promised land." It's a reasonable supposition, but it's also dead wrong.

A large segment of the population does not retain the services of a Financial Planner. As a consequence, they are not receiving the advice and guidance they so desperately need. The super-wealthy are getting more than enough help, but once you descend a little lower on the economic ladder, most people are on their own. Some haven't got a clue how to get from Point A to Point B, and some can't yet identify Points A and B. Others don't even attempt the journey or have just given up.

For a number of reasons, many middle-class households fail to seek professional advice and planning to help manage their savings, investments, and legacy planning. Some of these reasons are based on poor experiences with financial services professionals in the past; some are based on a lack of information or even misinformation; and some stem from a widespread reluctance among people in the U.K. to discuss personal finances with ... well, anyone – including spouses, partners, children, and grandchildren.

My philosophy is that people who need help should seek help, *especially* those who must be careful about matters financial, which is most of us. The affluent have no problems finding experts to provide them with bespoke financial advice and planning. In fact, such assistance usually seeks *them* out.

However, most of the people I enjoy serving – clients who are well-off but not mega-rich – are not seen as desirable clients by the private banks and investment houses that cater to the top 1 percent. As a result, the average middle-class household is not getting the kind of advice it needs. Instead, these households are receiving advice (if they're receiving any at all) from salespeople – from financial advisers whose main concern is selling financial products because that's how they earn their fees and commissions.

Historically, Financial Services Was Product-Oriented

Although the U.K. financial services profession has moved away in recent years from commission-based compensation to fee-based compensation, the industry is still product-sales-oriented. For that reason, most independent financial advisers are still product-oriented in one or more areas, and this is one of the biggest turn-offs to the non-super-rich. If you have "just" a half-million pounds to give as a legacy, which is not a lot when you consider current housing prices, the only advice you'll get from most financial advisers will be a few product-oriented recommendations. This is what most people have come to expect from *all* financial services professionals – a salesperson who will present them with a menu of options and a few words of "wisdom." They have thus resigned themselves to the "fact" that when they meet with an adviser, he or she will try to sell them something: a pension, a mortgage, or an annuity.

By contrast, financial planning offers benefits that extend far beyond those of a single product or group of products. For example, in and of itself, owning a life insurance policy is of limited value. The real value lies in knowing that if a claim is made, the right amount of money will go to the right people at the right time. The client or financial adviser can guess at this, but only a financial plan can quantify the amount of cover, type of cover, and duration of cover required, and can arrange an effective Trust solution in which the cover is held, allowing the money to pass to your chosen beneficiaries with minimal time and hassle and with greater protection of the funds for those beneficiaries. Likewise, the value of a pension contribution is not merely the tax relief provided, nor the chosen provider or underlying investments. It is the knowledge that the provisions you've put in place can deliver the kind of retirement you desire.

In short, buying a portfolio of financial products without developing concrete objectives and a strategic plan for accomplishing those objectives is like purchasing a collection of the finest carpentry tools without having any idea how to use them or what to build.

In my view, if you're successful but not mega-wealthy, and you're seeking the best financial *planning* advice available, you should hire someone whose income is *not* solely dependent upon selling financial products. In fact, the Financial Planner's fee structure is one of the first topics you should address when you interview candidates for the job.

At The Family Legacy Solution, we believe an independent Financial Planner should focus first and foremost on nurturing an ongoing advisory and planning relationship with each client. Although Financial Planners *do* earn fees on any products sold, this should be a secondary consideration for them – if it's a consideration at all. Considering the volume of investment information available online, as well as the number of good do-it-yourself investment services, there's no reason that most of you should feel obliged to purchase products from your Financial Planner. Because we at The Family Legacy Solution are paid separate fixed fees for our planning and advisory services, we feel no obligation to push financial products on our customers. It's a different story with financial advisers, however, because they are *not* usually reimbursed for any advice they offer during the course of selling products.

Beware Potential Conflicts of Interest

When dealing with an adviser or consultant whose remuneration depends upon product sales, one potential hazard for you (the customer) is that this adviser is also a salesperson. As such, he or she has a financial incentive to sell you more products, whether you need them or not.

A financial adviser's remuneration is often based on a percentage of your invested funds. If giving away capital is part of your legacy strategy, this might generate a conflict of interest, because such a strategy could substantially reduce the adviser's income. By contrast,

The Family Legacy Solution receives as payment a percentage of *all* assets owned by the family members with whom we work, thus removing any conflict of interest.

I'm not suggesting that most financial advisers succumb to conflicts of interest, continually selling you new products to generate additional fees and commissions for themselves (a practice known as "churning"), but it's been known to happen. Although most financial advisers behave ethically, the potential for conflicts of interest is something you should keep in mind when forming relationships with financial services professionals.

Even when a Financial Planner is remunerated for services rendered, rather than products sold, conflicts of interest can still arise. A planner's heart may be in the right place, but if his remuneration is based on a percentage of investable assets – a standard practice – there is a potential conflict of interest. If the investments the planner recommends perform well, he gets paid more, and so do you. An unscrupulous planner might therefore be tempted to take greater risks with your money than you'd like, in the hope of earning more money for himself. Conversely, he might take fewer risks than you'd like to prevent losses to his own income stream. A conflict of interest also might arise when a client wants to spend or donate money, as this would reduce the assets under management. Hence, it always pays to be vigilant – without being paranoid).

Before purchasing products and/or pursuing a different investment strategy, query your Financial Planner to determine whether the advice and products are truly in your best interest. When in doubt, feel free to solicit a second opinion from another financial services professional.

Most of the ongoing remuneration my colleagues and I receive at The Family Legacy Solution is not based on a percentage of clients' assets under management. Our ongoing fees are a percentage of net assets of the family, regardless of where they are invested. In addition, we charge fixed fees for each component of our planning package. This has the salutary effect of eliminating most conflicts of interest, but it sometimes makes it more difficult for us to help the very people who are most in need of planning. Because we invoice clients for advice and planning before the plans bear fruit, some prospective customers are unable to see past the fees. Although they are always enthused by the prospect of achieving financial independence – of launching second careers, devoting time to charitable causes, or taking cruises around the world – some balk at the fees. At the point when the fees are due, financial independence is sometimes still a few years away. It's still a bit abstract. But the fees? Those are tangible; they are here and now. So ironically, we sometimes lose clients because of our efforts to minimise potential conflicts of interest.

The Value of Financial Planning

One of my friends recently succeeded in losing 60 pounds, dropping from 17.5 to just over 13 stone in under a year. He'd been overweight for 15 years, but had done nothing about it. He'd long hoped to lose weight, and had dreamed of having a flat belly again, as well as pectorals the size of footballs. He tried almost every diet product hawked on television – pills, juice drinks, milkshakes, and packaged meals. Some of the products were obvious rubbish, but some have worked for other people. They didn't work for him, though, because he really had no plan for losing weight. He had no strategy or metrics to guide his use of these products and help him evaluate his progress. In fact, he had no idea how many calories he was consuming every day and, to be honest, he didn't want to know.

Weight loss "would be wonderful," but he had no sense of urgency about it until he developed severe foot pain from carrying around the extra pounds. *This* is what prompted him to "get real," to develop the specific and meaningful goal of eliminating chronic foot pain. *This* is what drove him to follow a simple weight-loss regimen recommended by his doctor. Finally, he began counting calories, eliminated junk food from his diet, and substituted smaller portions of healthy food in place of the "heaps of curry" he'd been eating every day.

From November 2011 until October 2012, he implemented the plan and *voilà*! It worked! It worked even better than he'd imagined. It worked *without* Herculean acts of willpower and punishing sacrifices. Talking with him today, he'll tell you that the most remarkable thing about the experience was not the weight loss, but how effortless the process became once the plan was developed and put into action. Once he set his goal and adopted the proper habits, the weight-loss plan took on a life of its own.

Just like my friend's diet products, financial products are merely a means to an end – one of several tools that can help you move from Point A to Point B.

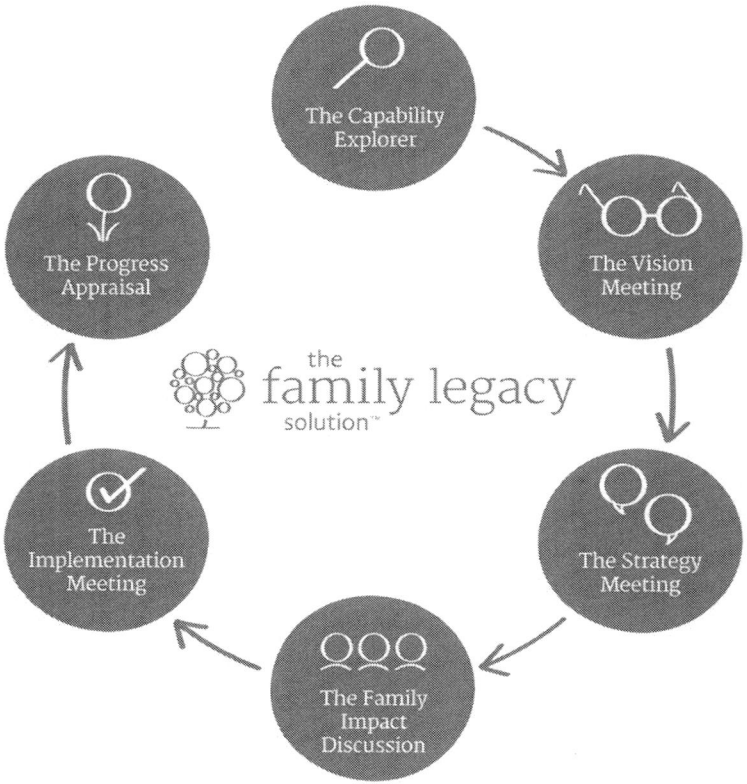

The most important thing is not the product, but understanding (A) where you are today; (B) where you want to be tomorrow; (C) how to achieve the goals; and (D) the implementation of the plan. It's only when you reach Phase D (implementation) that products enter into the equation.

The financial plan, along with the conversations that attend it, has more value than the products you choose. For example, we at the Financial Legacy Solution begin the planning process with what we call

Capability Exploration, followed by the Vision Meeting, the Strategy Meeting, the Family Impact Discussion, the Implementation Meeting, and the Progress Appraisal. Each of these process components helps you and your family identify goals and choose the best methods for achieving them.

Collectively, these components allow you and your Financial Planner to create a detailed blueprint for transporting you from where you are to where you want to be. Attempting to realise your personal and financial goals without this detailed set of blueprints is like attempting to lose weight without any idea of how to do that. It's like trying to build a skyscraper with nothing but piles of concrete, steel, glass, and some enthusiasm. And even if you succeed in erecting the office tower, it's unlikely the structure will be stable and enduring.

There is tremendous value in financial planning – in sorting out all the facts and figures in your life, and then evaluating the best ways to harness your resources to reach your goals.

Some people don't need financial planning. They know their situation inside and out, and have already mapped out the best route to their destination. But most people do need planning. Many have no idea how to design a plan, or how to even begin. Some come to us with shoeboxes or carrier-bags brimming with bits of paper – bank and pension statements, assorted receipts, insurance policies, and other documents.

That's fine.

A good Financial Planner will soon make sense of those bits of paper. It's not an ideal start, but the planner will know how to transform that mess into an evaluation of your assets and liabilities and, from there, into the basis for a strategic plan.

About a year ago, we worked with a couple who wanted to retire. They were of retirement age, but they'd done *nothing* to pave the way. They had their heads so firmly buried in the sand that their backsides were getting sunburnt. After sitting down with them, I said, "I understand all of your assets, so let's talk about your expenditures." They had *no clue* about their expenditures. They knew they were spending more money than they should be, and that they weren't saving, and they were embarrassed to admit it. So I said, "Okay, pay us

£300, and we'll work it out for you. Just give us all your bank and credit card statements for the last 12 months."

I had one of my administrative team members sift through each of these statements and classify them. When I returned to them with the results, I said, "This is what we've got you spending your money on. This is what your income is. This is what you're spending it on. This is what the shortfall is at the moment. And when you retire, this is the income you can expect from what you've already got – your pension plan and your state pension. We've adjusted some of the figures from what you've told us – for example, you might not be spending this in retirement, but you might be spending some other money on that. And this is the shortfall you've got there. And here is the shortfall if one of you dies tomorrow."

There were lots of bright red negative numbers at the bottom. It scared them, but it was a wake-up call, and they found the exercise incredibly valuable. As a result of learning what reality looked like, we are now preparing a plan for them.

Each financial planning component has value in and of itself, but the component that's *least* valuable is the products.

Choosing the Right Financial Planner

When searching for the best Financial Planner for your needs and personality, there are three things you should seek: a Good Relationship, Creativity, and Leadership.

A Good Relationship. You and your planner needn't become best friends, but you shouldn't hate spending time with the person, either. Your personalities and values should be a match – good enough that you will trust the person with your personal information. The planner should make you think, "If something goes wrong, she is here to help me. My spouse will be taken care of, and my kids will know how to sort things out." This is my rule of thumb for what constitutes a Good Relationship.

Creativity. You've got problems to solve, or you need paths to achieve your goals. Creativity and expertise are an integral part of what makes a good planner, as opposed to the adviser who will merely offer a limited menu of product options or a paint-by-numbers, one-size-fits-all plan.

Leadership. The right planner will tell you what you need to do – even if it's not what you really want to hear. He'll listen to who you are, and will tell you how to accomplish your visions. He'll eliminate the things you don't want, and help you accomplish things you *do* want.

Believe it or not, anyone can call himself a Financial Planner in the U.K., but that doesn't make him an expert adviser and asset manager. Regardless of how many words or initials follow someone's name, the designations that truly matter are *Chartered Financial Planner*, which is bestowed by the Personal Finance Society and is specific to the U.K., and *Certified Financial Planner*, which is granted by the Institute of Financial Planning (the U.K. administrator of the International Board of Standards and Practices for Certified Financial Planners). Financial planners who are members of these organisations must pass rigorous tests and commit to continuing professional development to retain those designations.

You can start your search for the right Financial Planner through these sites:

- The Personal Finance Society:
  www.thepfs.org/membership/findanadviser/
- The Institute of Financial Planning:
  www.financialplanning.org.uk/wayfinder/find-planner
- www.unbiased.co.uk
- www.vouchedfor.co.uk

Whilst someone with the Chartered Financial Planner and/or Certified Financial Planner designation isn't guaranteed to be a superstar, these certifications demonstrate a certain seriousness of purpose and commitment to excellence that someone without the designations may lack. At a minimum, someone with these designations is less of an "unknown quantity" than someone who hasn't bothered to take the exams and commit to ongoing professional development.

What questions should you ask when interviewing a Financial Planner? Here are the most basic questions that I can recommend:
1. How do you work with your clients?
2. Do you work with a certain type of client?
3. What are your qualifications?
4. What experience do you have?
5. Tell me about your team.
6. How do I pay you?
7. What services do you provide, and what don't you provide?
8. What is it like to be your client?

Red Flags: If the person's process doesn't revolve around a plan (i.e. solutions instead of products), continue your search. You should also look elsewhere if the planner doesn't work with people like you – people with similar backgrounds, incomes, and asset levels – or if the planner lacks significant experience, doesn't have a support team, or has no basic qualifications. And if the person can't be specific about how he or she is paid, or is dependent on selling products to generate income, you should run from the office instead of merely walking.

Green Flags: Good responses to the questions above include specific and documented approaches to the planning process; someone who works only (or predominantly) with a certain type of client – a client like you – and who has experience in working with this type of client. The planner should also have a support team that includes para-planners and other specialists, and should be a Chartered Financial Planner and/or a Certified Financial Planner. A good planner will thoroughly and transparently explain the fee structure, and should be happy to talk about what they do and what they don't do.

Do-it-yourself Tasks versus Tasks Best Left to Planners

Are there certain planning tasks that you can or should manage yourself, as well as tasks best managed by the Financial Planner? In other words, how much planning and product selection can you undertake yourself, if you want to?

This depends upon your skills, your background, and your comfort levels with various types of planning jobs, as well as the areas in which the planner specialises. Many Financial Planners specialise in particular areas such as legacy planning or retirement planning. Before you choose a planner, consider whether you want someone who's a generalist or someone who specialises in addressing specific needs or particular types of planning.

There isn't any one part of the planning process that is sacrosanct or that absolutely must be done by the planner. When it comes to setting up certain plans, the planner can act as more of a coach than a strategist and leader. It all depends on the complexity of your financial situation and the plan you need. Some plans are fairly easy to craft and implement, but may contain components for which you'll need additional expertise – such as "cash-flow projections." Even if you're familiar with cash-flow projections, you may need help with the plan's tax implications.

Don't make the mistake of thinking that, just because you understand how to use Excel software or another kind of financial planning software, that this makes you an expert.

I've had a couple of prospects say, "Why should I pay you several thousand pounds to do a plan, when I can do it myself on Excel?" The answer is that knowing how to use Excel does not qualify you as a Chartered Financial Planner. The reason you pay experts is not for the tools that they have at their disposal but for the knowledge, experience, and expertise they possess in the field. I know how to drive a car, but that doesn't mean I know how to assemble or repair one. Even if you're able to create a workable financial model, a proper model must be flexible, taking into account that if one variable changes, it may affect all the other variables. The moment you take these things into account, the complexity of that model on Excel becomes *frightfully* difficult.

Also, I wouldn't advise someone to save a few pounds by ignoring (or making superficial assumptions about) the legal implications of one component of a plan. This can be hazardous. Even if you're qualified to assemble a comprehensive plan, it couldn't hurt to consult with a Financial Planner to ensure you've covered every contingency – to make sure that the plan is "airtight." There are many areas in which you'd better make sure you know what you're doing.

That being said, there are plenty of tasks that clients can handle by themselves – or at least start by themselves. Budget planning and the collection of asset-liability information are two examples. Investment management is something that's become increasingly common – and will be even more common in the future. With the proliferation of financial information on the Internet, purchasing and managing your own investments has largely been demystified. While it couldn't hurt to consult with a Financial Planner to ensure that you've covered all the bases, today the average person can undertake a lot of the "heavy lifting."

In general, insurance policies are also a good do-it-yourself opportunity. Although complex insurance contracts require in-depth advice, a standard term insurance life policy is something most people can buy themselves. A good Financial Planner will say, "I'm happy for you to buy this yourself, as long as it works in conjunction with the overall plan."

If you say, "I'd like to do my own thing," and you buy products on the Web, that's fine with us. We just want to know where you've put the money so we have the ability to help you track its progress, particularly when it's review time – because we want to make sure it's invested in accordance with your risk-return profile. If you decide to become more cautious or more adventurous with your investment strategy, we'll want to know about that too, because it *will* change the fundamental contours of your plan.

The bottom line is: as long you don't go completely "off-script," and you allow us to engage in proper auditing and oversight, you can undertake any number of tasks yourself. We're perfectly happy with that. Any good Financial Planner will be happy to say that, because they are all about the plan, not just generating product sales.

Ultimately, it's possible for you to make mistakes at any time during the planning and implementation process, but by using the services of a Financial Planner you can eliminate (or at least dramatically reduce) the most common mistakes. The advice, counsel, and second opinions offered by a Financial Planner can be invaluable, even to the most knowledgeable persons.

2. Exploring Your Capabilities

ONCE YOU'VE SELECTED YOUR FINANCIAL planner, the next step is assessing your current situation. At The Family Legacy Solution, this evaluation of financial capabilities and commitments is known as The Capability Explorer.

We begin by quantifying your current assets – by determining how much money you have and where it's located. From there, we make an assumption about future rates of return (or growth rates) on your current investments relative to inflation, and we discuss this assumption with you to ensure that you're comfortable with it. It doesn't matter which rate of inflation is assumed, as that number can always be changed if circumstances warrant. What's paramount is not just the nominal number, but the performance/change in investments / income / expenditures relative to inflation.

For example, if your money is parked in a savings account, you can reasonably expect to make inflation. If it's invested in property, you'll probably make inflation plus one percent. And if the money is in an investment portfolio, the return will likely be inflation plus 1.5 to 2.5 percent. (Note: such returns are cautious medium- to longer-term expectations. Your short-term history may differ because of low interest rates, higher property valuations, or other factors.)

Again, if the actual inflation rate diverges from our assumption, that's not a problem. The only issue is whether the return on your assets meets expectations relative to inflation because – if you're still working – your income will rise with inflation. More often than not, unless the economy is experiencing a meltdown, your earnings will *surpass* inflation. If you're already retired, we address payment increases to which you are entitled each year. Some pensions don't increase their payments in response to inflation; others rise with inflation but are capped at a certain amount. We also look at the percentage to which a spouse would be entitled if the retiree should die. Typically it's 50 percent, but sometimes it's as much as two-thirds and sometimes it's as little as zero.

We look at state pensions, both pre- and post-retirement, to determine what you're going to receive and whether you'll be affected by pending changes, e.g. changes to the state pension age and movement to a flat-rate payment. If you are still working, we make an allowance for continuing service if applicable. For example, if you've been enrolled in a defined-benefit scheme for 10 years and you're still with the employer, they will give you a forecast based upon accrual-type points. We'll assess what you'll receive if you quit today versus continuing to work for another x years based on your current salary and any expected salary increases.

If you've got a money-purchase pension fund, we'll project the future fund value, given expectations for growth plus your expected contributions. We use current annuity rates and an adjustment for the lump-sum you could take to project your future pension income.

To evaluate your liabilities, we follow much the same process – only in reverse.

In addition to quantifying current assets and forecasting growth rates relative to inflation, as well as helping you value and understand your pension benefits and options, your Financial Planner should:

- ☐ Review your core expenditures and discretionary spending – a review that should include recurring and future lump-sum expenditures.
- ☐ Work with you to make projections based on various "what-if" scenarios – death, illness, early retirement, etc.
- ☐ Help you overcome any discomfort about discussing finances with your spouse and other family members.

Involve Your Spouse/Partner in the Process

The last point – a reluctance to discuss money and finances with spouses, partners, and other family members – may seem trivial. However, it can be a major impediment to effective legacy planning, not to mention the timely and efficient transfer of assets to beneficiaries. This is especially true when one member of a married couple is responsible for managing the finances and the other isn't involved at all – to the point where he or she doesn't even know where to find key documents.

Here's where I put my foot down. Regardless of a client's reluctance to discuss finances with family members, I insist that spouses/partners (and often the children) be involved in the legacy planning process to some extent. The most common objections I encounter from clients are that they don't want their children to realise what they might inherit; they don't trust their sons- or daughters-in-law; they worry about creating a rift among the children (some of whom they view as spendthrifts who are likely to spend the inheritance before it's received), or they don't trust their husbands or wives. For these and other reasons, some clients want to avoid involving their families in the financial and legacy planning process.

At a minimum, your spouse/partner must be involved in the process. If not, you risk jeopardising his or her financial well-being for a considerable length of time.

The classic example of such jeopardy is when the husband deals with all of the finances and then dies or is taken ill – stroke, heart attack, etc. – leaving the wife and children with no idea where the money is or how to deal with it when they find it. Often, the husband hasn't thought ahead to "What happens when I'm not around?" and has compounded the problem by not drawing up an effective Will or failing to grant power-of-attorney to his wife.

We help avoid these situations by talking about this scenario and engaging in creative problem-solving during the Capability Explorer stage. We find out what the barriers are by asking, "Why, Mr. Husband, do you not want to bring your wife into this conversation? She doesn't have to be interested; she doesn't have to take over. Please understand that if you die first or something happens to you, everything is going to land on her plate. What's your contingency plan for that? Why haven't you involved her with that? Is it because she's just not interested, for whatever reason? Why don't you want to engage your children? Is it because you don't want them to squabble over their inheritance? We can find ways around these problems."

So, for example, we might say to a client, "You could tell the children as much or as little as you want. You could tell them, 'We realise we've put away more money than we're likely to need. If we could provide you with some funds now, how would this benefit you?' You're not suggesting anything; you're not telling them how much money you have. You don't *have* to tell them how much money you've got. You could just say, 'If something happens – if I'm struck down by lightning or something and I die – there's a box under the bed in the spare bedroom with two keys to it. I've got one, and here's the other. All the financial documents are in the box. Go and open the box.' That's it. You don't have to do anything else. You don't have to tell them anything more than that."

We say to all of our clients, "You need to have a secure firebox or safe in which you keep all your main documents – even seemingly insignificant things like passwords to online accounts. (It's not ubiquitous *yet* for clients above a certain age, but for younger people, it's fairly standard that they access their financial accounts online. Whether investment accounts, or even banks, there's sometimes no physical branch to visit these days.)

More than once, I've seen situations in which one spouse is suddenly struck down by an illness or dies, and the spouse isn't able to access the money, even with the legal power to do so. Even with power-of-attorney, even with a properly executed Will that grants them the power of executor, they can't *actually* access the money from the accounts because they don't have the requisite passwords or other information to do it. The surviving spouse can't simply call up the institution and access the accounts without a password. When she tries, the institution usually responds with, "We want a marriage certificate; we want identification for you; we want other proof of who you are." Even if the surviving spouse is a joint account holder, many financial institutions won't grant access to the money right away.

Budget Planning

After identifying your assets and liabilities, the next step in producing a structured financial plan is a thorough analysis of your incomes and expenditures – both now and what they are likely to be in the future. The best place to start is to produce a summary that details your present income broken down by source – whether this is a salary, pension, investment income, or other source. Due consideration must be given to how secure this income is. For example, income from a rental property could change if a tenant were to vacate.

In addition to your income, you need to consider your current expenditures. Here I prefer to use a system that considers expenditures in three distinct sections.

Core: bills that are likely to continue indefinitely. It's vital to consider all your regular monthly expenditure items. Most people start by listing what I term "core" expenditures, i.e. those coming out of their bank account every month. Some examples include:

- Rent
- Food, drink, and household products
- Building and contents insurance premiums
- Utility bills
- Travel and transportation expenses, vehicle, fuel, etc.

It's also important to budget for items that people consider one-off, lump-sum payments that come due when the need arises. These expenditures are often habitual in nature, and whilst they may not occur every year, a prudent budget plan must consider them. Examples include:

- Car depreciation
- White goods
- Property maintenance

Financial are expenditures relating to a specific financial asset such as a mortgage or insurance premiums. Financial commitments are likely to either change or cease in the future – e.g., mortgage payments at the end of the term of the loan or pension contributions at retirement. They can also be subject to clear and identifiable forces outside of your control, such as changes in interest rates.

Imagine you currently own a car valued at £5,000. If you were to replace that car today, you'd likely spend a total of £10,000. However, it is also likely that you will *actually* replace the vehicle in (say) three years' time, when your vehicle may have depreciated to £2,000 in value. At that time, the equivalent car would still cost £10,000 (inflation adjusted), meaning you would need to find £8,000 to replace your car, rather than the £5,000 it would cost you today. This £8,000 lump sum can be incorporated into your budget planner by dividing the £8,000 by three (the number of years until you replace your vehicle) and then again by 12 to convert it into a monthly expenditure. Therefore, you would need to save £222.23 per month over three years to cover the cost of upgrading the car.

At some point, such expenditures *will* arise, whether it's redecorating to maintain the value of your property or replacing the washing machine, so it's important that you budget for them.

Discretionary: all other expenditures – mainly those that could be forsaken if circumstances dictate. Examples include holidays and gifts.

In my experience, the above budgeting approach provides you with a more thorough and accurate analysis compared with, say, merely listing direct debit payments. If you produce a proper budget, which includes all of your possible expenditures, it reduces the risk of facing a cash shortfall when you need to replace an item such as a television. Having such an understanding is vital, both for people who are dependent upon living within either a fixed pension or variable investment income, and for those who are yet to retire but seeking to maximise their long-term savings.

Frequently, new clients overlook a number of habitual expenditures that are incurred on an irregular basis. Examples include the cost of replacing household goods or the depreciation on a motor vehicle. Not including such items within your budget planner will often result in an overestimation of your ability to save or, if you're living off your savings, an underestimation of the regular withdrawals needed from an investment strategy.

You should also prepare for the future by extending your budget plan to incorporate various "what-if" possibilities. These could include changes in your income and expenditures once you've retired or if you became sick – or even if you or your spouse/partner were to die. Doing this allows you to view your situation in such "what if" circumstances, helping you identify situations that might cause financial difficulties. Once you're able to identify these "what-if" scenarios, you can examine options to alleviate any shortfalls they might cause.

Please note that a budget plan is not designed to restrict you. It should be completed with the knowledge that the plan will constantly change as your situation evolves. The budget is a starting point for evaluating your current situation – one that will help you build a foundation for financial planning. Everyone should complete a budget plan regardless of their stage in life. Doing so will help identify your capacity for saving *before* retirement and determine how much investment income you'll need *after* retirement. A proper budget plan significantly reduces the need to tap into "rainy day" funds. Once these funds are depleted, your only likely option is to reduce your standard of living.

There are many different methods of creating a budget plan, as well as different ways to create a budget summary, using either a pen and paper or a software spreadsheet. The Money Advice Service website provides a good option:
https://www.moneyadviceservice.org.uk/en/categories/budget-planner

Budget planning doesn't have to be complicated, and the process will give you the confidence and ideas needed to adequately prepare for your future and that of your family.

Budgeting Your Time

Another issue with which I help my clients is overcoming "time deficits," i.e. helping them identify any undesirable activities that currently occupy much of their time. Together, we then pinpoint options to reduce or eliminate the time spent at these tasks while increasing the time devoted to more rewarding pursuits. Created by The Strategic Coach® (founded by Dan Sullivan), this idea is called the Activity Inventory™.

To develop the Activity Inventory, we ask clients to write down one sentence or a couple of words describing everything they do in a typical month – from chores to things they love doing, including hobbies or favorite activities and other interests. We ask them to be as thorough as they like, and to take as long as they want to do this.

As a participant, you'll walk around for a month, writing these things down, whether it's putting out the rubbish, washing the car, mowing the lawn, or taking the grandchildren out. Once you've created the list, in the margins, you will write down the numbers (1), (2), (3) or (4) next to each of these activities. Write the number (4) next to each activity that you're no good at doing or that you hate doing. Write the number (3) next to something if that activity isn't particularly unpleasant but isn't very rewarding. Write the number (2) next to something if you're pretty skilled or talented at the thing, but it's not something you look forward to doing. Jot down the number (1) next to an activity only if it's something you're really great at doing and it's something you love doing.

After you've compiled this list, we will sit down with you to examine the numbers, working out options to eliminate most (or all) of the *fours*, *threes* and *twos* and to increase the time spent pursuing the *ones*. We look at each item and ask you, "Does this have to be done? If so, is there someone else in the family or household who could do this instead of you?"

"No, I'm still the best person to do it."

"Well, if this has to be done, but you don't like doing it, can we *hire* someone to do it?" (Note: this person's fee should be added to the Budget Extender.)

The purpose of this exercise is to help you overcome "time deficits" regarding your favourite and least-favourite activities. After all, a key reason for seeking financial independence (and a key benefit of being financially independent) is not just to buy more "stuff" but also to buy yourself more time to do the things you love. So as part of the budget plan, we work on helping you achieve more "temporal freedom" along with financial freedom.

One of my biggest clients is so "time poor" that it hurts. Unfortunately, he's not in great health, and his wife's also in declining health. He has a fascinating life story, which I know he wants to record in writing. He also wants to spend more time with his wife and do more things together. But he currently spends a lot of time mowing his lawn and completing a list of other chores, even though it often annoys him. So we recently asked him, "Look, if you had someone to do all the gardening and other chores, how much would that cost?" And we showed him that they can afford to do that. We demonstrated that the couple can *afford to buy more time*.

Of course, once in a while, we encounter people who wouldn't know what to do with free time if they had it – and some already do. They tend to fill up their time with chores and errands through force of habit. As Financial Planners, we can't force people to pursue activities they might find more enjoyable. We can only help them to find the extra time.

The Consequences of Not Creating a Budget

A lot of fear and loathing is associated with budget preparation. Many people detest the very idea of going over bank statements, bills, and spreadsheets. Because of this, a *very* substantial number don't create written budgets. In my experience, the most common reasons for not creating a budget involve:

Time. Along with the idea that it's a dull and tedious task, budget preparation also requires a substantial time commitment. It's not something that can be done in a few minutes. Of course, you can hire a Financial Planner to do most of the work, but you cannot hire the person to do *all* of the work. Some participation is mandatory on your part.

Fear of Constraints. Some people believe that, once they determine how much needs to be saved and spent every week/month/year, they will be shackled to these saving and spending targets for life. That isn't necessarily true. Budget plans are *not* designed to restrict families. They are designed to highlight the current reality, so that reality can eventually be amended and reshaped to suit your liking. If you're spending every penny you take in, and have no realistic year-to-year savings plan in place, at some point reality is going to intrude. And without budget planning, that reality is likely to be an unpleasant one. It's your choice: you can keep doing what you're doing now and hope for the best, or take control of your finances and assume greater control over your future.

A Preference for "Blissful" Ignorance. In some instances, people don't want to admit to a Financial Planner how much they're spending and on what. This is rather silly when you consider that budgets and Financial Planners are designed to help you, not judge you. You're only cheating yourself if you live in denial – if your mantra becomes "I don't spend that kind of money on *those things*." You'll really let yourself down with that attitude. Yes, you'll identify areas in which you could/should be spending less, but you may also identify areas in which you could be spending more.

Put simply, the failure to undertake a thorough budget analysis is likely to undermine your ability to achieve your goals. A few obvious outcomes of failing to create a budget include:

- Your lifestyle expenditures, without any previous forethought, may expand to match an increase in your disposable income. This will dramatically reduce your capacity to save.
- You may underestimate or overestimate how much income you will need in retirement.
- You may remain unaware of the implications of rising mortgage interest costs upon your ability to continue to meet your basic expenditures.
- You may fail to quantify how much income you would need if you became unable to work because of ill health or injury. This could cause you to be under-insured or over-insured.

Not producing a budget plan can have a significant impact upon your future. It can mean you will not have the funding available in retirement to accomplish everything you wish. It could even force you to work longer than you had previously expected.

Let's say, for example, that a 45-year-old man doesn't have a working budget plan and, as a result, is currently spending all of his disposable income. He is 20 years away from retirement. After following a budget planning exercise, he now realises that he can afford to cut back his expenditures on non-essential items by £100 per month. By saving this £100 per month over the remaining 20 years until retirement, he could build a fund equal to £42,863.10 (with five percent annual compound return) by the time he is 65. If he now used this fund to arrange a Purchased Life Annuity, which provides a guaranteed income for life, this would supply him with a gross income at the outset equal to £2,596.80 per year, given current annuity rates. As a result, not only does our hypothetical retiree have an extra £216.40 income per month in retirement funds, he also now realises that he needs £100 less per month for expenditures – for an overall combined increase of £316.40 per month in disposable retirement income.

The example above highlights the advantages of producing a budget when planning for your retirement. Doing so will give you greater confidence in your ability to save, providing you with a lot more opportunities for the future. It also reduces the possibility of reaching retirement without sufficient funds to accomplish everything you want to do.

It is *always* better to produce a budget plan that is as accurate as possible, with scope for it to change if/when your circumstances change.

Avoid These Common Mistakes

While exploring your capabilities and preparing a budget, alone or in tandem with a Financial Planner, you'll want to avoid costly mistakes. The most common of these is failing to produce a budget plan in the first place, followed by:

Denial: Be honest. Don't lie to yourself or your Financial Planner about your current circumstances. The two most common examples I encounter are: (1) clients who don't want to tell me about an asset, because they're under the impression that I'm a financial adviser – i.e. I'm going to try to sell them something to earn a commission – and (2) clients who don't reveal all of their expenditures because they're embarrassed about how they spend their money – i.e. they're worried that I'll condemn them as "spendthrifts."

As often as not, people are likely to put up smokescreens when it comes to their liabilities rather than their assets. If anything, they worry that they don't have enough assets to interest me in becoming their planner. They'll say, "I'm sure you don't want to deal with me. I've only got half a million. I'm sure you've got much bigger clients than me." The answer is, "Yes, I have bigger clients than you, but we wouldn't be talking if I weren't interested in working with you."

Inaccurate Assumptions. One of the biggest mistakes made by clients is overestimating the likely growth rates of their investments and/or failing to link those growth rates to inflation. We always say to clients, "We're going to *over*estimate on the expenses – on the amounts you're spending, as well as your liabilities." We assume that interest rates will go up faster than they probably will. At the same time, we try to *under*estimate increases in returns on investments – for example, on property. It's better to make conservative estimates and be pleasantly surprised than to underestimate expenses and overestimate returns, and then find yourself faced with shortfalls.

One of the worst assumptions someone can make is using past returns as a guide to future earnings. This is a classic mistake. Someone will look at what other investors made in the last five years or so, and simply assume that they can expect the same results. Making projections based on past returns is of no use whatsoever. It's for this reason that so many of the documents issued by financial services institutions contain disclaimers that read, "Past performance is not a guide for the future and may not be repeated." For now, the only assumption one can make based on past performance is that the sun will (probably) rise in the east and then set in the west.

Another common mistake is to assume that expenditures will remain the same in post-retirement as they are today. Keep in mind that once you retire, you will not be commuting to work every day, so your petrol bills will go down. And if you have two cars at the moment, you might want to "downsize" to a single car. Conversely, you will likely spend *more* money on items where you didn't previously – e.g., on holidays. This is why it's important to retest your assumptions and to underestimate returns and overestimate expenses. If you don't, you'll likely find that you're continually dipping into your capital, which could cause the capital to be irreversibly eroded. And, if you'd foreseen this at the outset, you could have implemented another strategy that would have given you a more secure income for that ongoing need. (Or perhaps you could have reduced your expenditures.)

Inadequate Research. This includes everything from not knowing your pension's spousal entitlement to – believe it or not – not knowing where your assets are. (Frankly, some people just forget. Others lose track.)

Failing to Update the Budget, or Doing So in an Inconsistent Way. In addition to regularly reviewing and updating the budget plan, it's important to be consistent. By "consistent" I mean that when you review and update the plan, you go back and test your assumptions again according to the same criteria and formulas: Are the old assumptions still valid? There's no point in saying, "Inflation's at three percent, so a fair rate of interest rate on my debts is six percent, but I'm going to assume a fifteen percent return on my longer-term investments." That's not a consistent approach to financial planning.

At this early stage of the financial planning process, you can take heart in knowing that budgeting is the most difficult part. For the reasons mentioned above, most people don't like doing it, but budgeting is probably the most vital part of the process, so it's crucial that you be honest and thorough. Of course, if you're working with a Financial Planner, he or she can do much of the heavy lifting for you. Very often, our clients hand us a boxful of papers, and we take it from there. As long as you provide adequate information, we say, "Just give us your bank and credit card statements and we'll work through it for you." It's quite labour-intensive for us, so it's not something we offer freely. And we *do* want you to participate in the process to some extent.

Spendthrifts and Hoarders

One of the most common excuses for failing to prepare a budget (or undertake any financial planning) is "I can never save for this or that, because we've got so little income." The irony is that the whole purpose of financial planning in general, and budget planning in particular, is helping people *find ways to save and invest their income*, regardless of how much they have.

People who claim they can't budget and save because they don't have enough money remind me of the story of the lumberjack. An old lumberjack is busy felling trees with an antique axe when someone asks, "Why don't you buy a chainsaw so you can take down 100 times as many trees in the same time? To this the lumberjack replies, "I'm too busy cutting down trees to buy a chainsaw."

In the vast majority of cases, people who aren't saving at least a few pounds per week are victims of their own self-fulfilling prophecies. They aren't saving money because they haven't budgeted for it, and even when presented with the opportunity to create a budget, they claim they don't have enough money to justify the budget planning.

Even if you're struggling to keep pace with your financial obligations today, there's a good chance that these obligations will decrease as you approach retirement age, giving you more disposable income that can be devoted to savings and investments. For example, as your children grow and leave the household, you'll be spending less on food, clothing, transportation, and utilities. The same holds true of mortgages. Unless you've taken on more debt that you could ever repay, at some point you're going to pay off your loans, freeing up a portion of your income for other things. If you're like many people, you may have become so accustomed to certain expenditures that it's never crossed your mind that someday these expenses will decrease or disappear entirely.

On the reverse side of this coin are people who are so accustomed to saving and accumulating that they're unable to enjoy the fruits of financial independence even after they've attained it. Remember, one common goal of financial planning is not to retire at or near age 65, but to achieve financial independence at the earliest possible age. At the point where you no longer have to work for money ever again, you've achieved this goal. If I'm talking to someone who's in pre-retirement, and I can show them that they are already financially independent, this means they can retire *now* – if they choose. By focusing less on retirement at a set age and more on financial independence at *any* age, I encourage people to make more informed decisions about what they want to do with their lives. Someone who has reached 65 should already be financially independent, or very close to it. If not, they are probably in a bit of trouble.

If you think you may be nearing financial independence but you aren't sure, it's time to produce a budget to determine where you stand. If you've already achieved financial independence, but you're a bit of an accumulator – someone who can't break the habit of saving and investing and almost never spending anything – it's time to visit a Financial Planner to start making *the most* of that money instead of simply making *more* money.

At The Family Legacy Solution, we've developed step-by-step approaches to help both "hoarders" and "spendthrifts" plan more productive and enjoyable futures. What we've found is that you can't get people to change overnight the habits of a lifetime. It simply doesn't work.

Our remedy for hoarders is to give them a small taste of financial freedom. Typically, we locate some surplus capital and say, "Let's take some capital from here and transfer it to a new account – a 'play account'." The sum will be relatively modest relative to their situation, but large enough to be meaningful. Then we suggest purchases, usually items drawn from their wish lists, on which they can spend this money.

With spendthrifts, our typical approach begins with identifying a small expenditure that they can forgo. We then divert the money they would have spent on this item into a savings or investment instrument, and encourage them to watch (and enjoy) as the pot grows over time.

One of my clients is a retired couple. They've got a few hobbies, as well as a wish list. At this point in their lives, there's no reason they can't tick off everything on that wish list. In fact, when I visit them next, I think they'll be surprised about just how many things they can afford to do.

However, because they're hoarders, I know that if I simply give them the financial plan and say, "Congratulations. See you later. Any questions, give us a call," they might not do anything on the list. I'll need to work with them. I'll need to start by saying, "Pick one or two of the items at the top of your list, and let's focus on doing those." If I were to leave such clients to their own devices, most wouldn't feel comfortable with the numbers. They wouldn't trust the numbers alone. We could assure them that they have more than enough money to fulfill every goal. We could tell them this until we were blue in the face, and it wouldn't make the slightest difference.

However, if we can effectively say, "You said this year that you were going to spend £100,000 on a cumulative series of activities, but you only spent £20,000 on a handful of those activities so let's keep going; you can afford it." That might make a difference. We might have to keep going back and urging the couple to spend the next £20,000 in the following year, and then another £20,000 in the year after that, but eventually the job will get done. Left to their own devices, they would never have the courage to spend the entire £100,000 upfront, but with persistent and gentle encouragement, we can prompt such people to complete their wishes.

Far from being an exercise to dread, Capability Exploration and budget planning are activities you should look forward to. Capability Exploration and budgeting can make abstract goals and ambitions come to life by assigning them a realistic "start date." For me, this is one of the most satisfying parts of my job.

2A: *The Capability Explorer*

The Capability Explorer helps you organise and list your resources and commitments. It covers your personal information, children and dependents, employment details, income and expenditures and anticipated changes to your financial situation. We will work with you to list your assets (residence and other property, liquid assets, and details of your investments, savings, and business assets). We'll go through details of your liabilities, along with retirement planning, pensions, and other benefits. Together we develop a detailed list of your insurance arrangements – including life, health, and illness insurance – and we'll help you explore details of your health, lifestyle, and legacy planning. We offer detailed descriptions of the various levels of your attitude toward investment risk, from very conservative to very aggressive.

We have detailed forms and guides available for you online at
thefamilylegacysolution.co.uk

2B: The Budget Extender

The Budget Extender helps you list all of your expenditures.

The Budget Extender process examines income, expenditures, commitments, and discretionary expenditures – currently and in retirement – for you and your partner, and compares anticipated situations should either of you outlive the other.

You can find detailed forms online from our website at
thefamilylegacysolution.co.uk

3. Breathing Life into Visions and Goals

SOMETIMES THE BIGGEST OBSTACLE TO effective legacy planning is lack of motivation. When I query new clients about their visions for the future, I often discover that they have no specific goals. Other than saving money and/or increasing the value of their portfolios, they haven't given much thought to specific, meaningful goals they wish to accomplish. Some have never considered how they could harness their money to make their dreams come true. It's hardly surprising, therefore, that people without actionable goals would be uninterested in designing financial and legacy plans. Why plan for getting from Point A to Point B if you haven't established where Point B is – or determined why you should even care about getting there?

I'm not suggesting that these people have no imagination or ambition. Most often, the reason people fail to develop specific goals is because they've long considered such goals to be out of reach. By the time a Financial Planner breaks the news that they *do* (or *will*) have the resources needed to accomplish such goals, they're taken by surprise, and often need both time and encouragement to reanimate their "vision-quest muscles." Whenever I encounter these people, I ask them to consider the financial and non-financial impact that financial planning can have on their families and communities. This can go a long way towards inspiring them.

Among other things, financial planning and legacy planning can help you to:

- ☐ Retire earlier.
- ☐ Pursue more rewarding work.
- ☐ Do more of the things that you enjoy.
- ☐ Try exciting new things such as travel.
- ☐ Pay for deposits on property.
- ☐ Repay mortgages.

- ☐ Fund grandchildren's educations.
- ☐ Assist charitable and other non-profit organisations.
- ☐ Contribute money and time to the community.
- ☐ Help others while you're still alive.
- ☐ Involve family in the financial planning and education process.
- ☐ Strengthen family bonds.
- ☐ Pass down your experience, skills, and values.
- ☐ Help those who are less fortunate while forging an attitude of gratitude for yourself and your loved ones.
- ☐ Achieve some tax savings.

Money has no intrinsic value. Its value lies in buying precious time and experiences, as well as material possessions.

Set Your Sights High!

Legacy planning involves more than identifying suitable investment products. It involves developing and implementing realistic visions and strategies and a financial plan. Health and time permitting, most visions *can* be realised, given adequate resources and planning. A common mistake is not setting the vision high enough. One of the biggest mistakes people make during Family Legacy Solution Vision Meetings is not allowing their imaginations to roam freely. We encourage people to go further and further with their visions.

Some people require very little prodding to dream big and spend big. Their attitude is, "We've built all this money up, so let's go spend it!" In other cases, one would need a pair of pliers to pry open the person's wallet – he just can't seem to set his goals higher than a molehill. I think the latter mindset stems from having lived within tight boundaries for so long, because it's a very common one. However, because the mind is a bit like a sponge, with enough coaching, many people eventually absorb new ideas and become excited about pursuing these opportunities that financial independence can provide.

I'm about to revisit a married couple in their mid-60s with no children. I've already performed some analyses for them, from which I've concluded that they could easily double their expenditures for the rest of their lives and still not worry about money. Hitherto, their idea of "splurging" on a hobby was to buy a motorhome. That wasn't a bad start, but they could do so much more to enjoy their surplus income.

To date, however, their response to my suggestions has been, "We're not interested."

"Okay, but are you *sure* this is all you want? Are you sure you don't want to donate anything to charity? If you could die with one pound left in the bank, would that be fine?"

"Yes."

"Well, how are you going to go through all the money? You're not really getting much value or enjoyment from the money so far."

It's not my mission to *force* clients into spending money on worthwhile people or causes, even if they otherwise have no idea what to do with it, but I'm very persistent about offering suggestions. In many cases, people eventually realise that they, and others, could be getting more value from the money – that the only things holding them back are old habits and mindsets, especially among people who are used to having little free time.

Common Mistakes in Goal-Setting

Another obstacle to developing specific visions is the preconceived notion that many people have regarding the *timing* of retirement and financial independence. A significant number assume that financial independence and retirement are inextricably linked to the dates set in pension schemes. In other words, they believe they must wait until they are at/near a certain age, usually the age at which the state pension begins distributing the funds, before they can begin serious goal-setting. I often meet new clients who say, "I've got this pension plan with XYZ insurance company [or with an old employer for whom I no longer work]. The benefits don't begin until age 65." That's the age that was set either by this individual when he took out the plan or by the company for which he no longer works, and it has nothing to do with when a financially independent individual is "allowed" to retire.

There is *nothing* to prevent most people from taking pension money as early as age 55. Yes, there may be a penalty for doing so, but that doesn't mean that you absolutely *must* continue working in your current job for another 10 or 15 years.

Please, don't postpone retirement until some preconceived date. Don't believe that you can't retire until the government begins paying your state pension or you reach a ripe old age. That is pure nonsense. A date had to be put on a pension scheme, either by the government or the pension company. It's not a mandatory retirement date, nor is it a deadline before which you are not allowed to retire.

A second common mistake is underestimating your longevity. Too many people worry about dying young instead of living to a very old age. This concern is understandable but, from a financial planning perspective, the greatest danger is that you'll live much longer than expected and your money will run out. Unfortunately, many people don't think of that.

When we find that someone has a money purchase pension plan, a personal pension, and we investigate their options of how to take that pension, which would include level income versus rising income, or providing income for a spouse, we normally see that the more options available, the lower the rate of income they'll receive at the start. Most people want all the money they can get immediately. Typically, we have to apply the brakes. "If you take too much money today, there could be too little in the future. Yes, your expenditures may be higher now, when you're in your early retirement years, than when you're in your 70s and early 80s, but ultimately, we have to ensure that this money lasts longer than you do."

In point of fact, I've never worked with a legacy-planning client whose money ran out. However, my colleagues and I *have* dealt with prospective clients who were pretty far gone.

We work with a married couple in their 70s who retired early. When we first met them, they'd been retired for about 10 years. After examining their situation, we said, "If you carry on at this rate, there's a high risk that in another 10 years, all the money will be gone." We discussed this topic extensively until I finally said, "There are three options you could pursue: You could spend less now, taking a smaller withdrawal to make things more sustainable. Or you could take *more* risk with your money. Or you could just accept the situation."

In the end, we pursued the first two strategies after conducting a budget plan exercise.

The clients told us, "We could easily save £100 or £200 a month of what we're spending." This allowed us to reduce their annual withdrawal by that amount. However, following the budget analysis, we realised that they needed to secure some of their income, so we took some of the pot and secured it with an insurance product that guaranteed them income for life. Even if the investment fell to zero, the income would continue.

This was quite expensive, and it isn't something I normally choose for most clients. However, because the client had an investment pot of about £200,000 and was withdrawing £14,000 a year (they later reduced that to about £10,000), we were in a difficult position. We believed they needed to withdraw only about £5,000 to live comfortably, so we took the £200,000 and split it in half. We kept drawing £5,000 from one half, just as you would a conventional investment, because that was paying for the things they wanted to do, and then we secured the rest with the insurance contract.

We suspected the uninsured investment would run out over time, but they were now assured that the other investment would pay £5,000 a year forever. The cost on the insured investment was about 1.2 percent more per annum than the other, but the £5,000 income would continue, and if the pot happened to grow (which it did) they could lock in a higher level of income.

Obviously, these clients made another mistake when it came to casting their vision and goals – setting objectives that their resources could not support. However, it's hardly a common mistake. In fact, I rarely encounter people who do that. Instead, I tend to encounter people with *surplus* assets.

Other common mistakes made at the Vision Meeting stage include:
- ☐ Allowing inertia to carry you along – e.g., going with the same flow that has always carried you along (routines, habits, and expectations) instead of proactively planning and dreaming for a better future.
- ☐ Not investigating your options.

How do you know what your options are? Here's where the Financial Planner can be of great value. At The Family Legacy Solution, for example, we use cash modelling projections to show you the outcomes of various "what if" scenarios. In other words, we show you what would happen if you withdrew *x* amount of money from your investments versus *y* amount. This allows you to determine the optimal sums that you can remove on a regular basis and prevents you from running out of money. It also helps us determine what levels of risk you can realistically tolerate with the investments. For example, we can determine that, if you take *this* level of risk, you'll likely receive *that* level of return, and we will then discuss how this could impact your daily situation and long-term goals. We can visit any number of scenarios to help you make more informed decisions.

Identifying Opportunities, Threats and Resources

Our approach to helping you create your vision and goals focuses on identifying opportunities, threats, and resources. Our clients follow a process of listing and evaluating specific opportunities, which are then matched with potential obstacles to the goals, as well as available resources that could help overcome these threats and grab the opportunities. To guide people through the table, we engage in a question-and-answer session that typically opens with a question known as The R-Factor Question®. Developed by Strategic Coach®, the question is usually phrased, "If we were sitting here three years from today, looking back over that period, what has to have happened during that time for you to feel happy with your progress?"

We use this question very often, usually at the start of the Vision Meeting. Our objective is prompting you to set your sights on the future rather than your current situation – to look forward instead of at the present or past. By eliciting answers that reflect what's truly important to you, we give you greater perspective. We do this by asking you to travel to some future moment – to imagine that you are already living a particular dream or goal, so that your imagination is not restricted by concerns about how the goal can be achieved. Too often, people self-censor their visions because past circumstances conditioned them to the idea that "this or that ambition is unlikely to happen because ..." Even when their financial circumstances change radically, many people remain stuck on these old mental paths. They default to the habit of saying to themselves, "I'd *love* to be able to open a yoga studio or pursue my hobby of restoring classic cars, but I can't because I don't have the time/money/freedom ..." By using the process described above, we place you at a mental point where your goals have already been accomplished and you are looking backward to *how* they were accomplished. This makes it more difficult to invent excuses about why you could not accomplish those goals. In your mind, you've already accomplished them. The boundaries have been erased and the hurdles overcome. You're merely engaged in a "post-game analysis."

It's important to use appropriate timescales when doing these exercises. With older clients, I wouldn't ask, "If we were sitting here 10 years from now ..." because the client's response might be, "I could be dead in 10 years." Discussing goals to be accomplished over very long timescales can be counterproductive, so we tend to use three years. This is long enough to accomplish quite a lot, but not so long that the scenarios become too distant or abstract.

Another purpose of the exercises is to help you identify what's really important, so you can assign priorities. This is why we ask questions at the outset of the planning process. We want to see what presses your buttons and what floats your boat.

To that end, another question we often ask is, "What's important to you about money?"

"Money gives me security."

"What's important to you about security?"

"It means I can pay the bills."

"Why is it important for you to pay the bills?"

"To avoid losing my current lifestyle. I've worked hard to get where I am."

We keep this dialogue going until we acquire a deep understanding of your fears and aspirations, priorities and values, risk tolerance and personal goals. In many instances, we ask questions that you've never been asked before. These may prompt you to become more introspective and self-aware. In effect, we tease out a rough psychometric profile that enables us to design financial and legacy plans custom-tailored to your desires. It also allows us to direct you toward visions and goals you might have abandoned, or forgotten about, but which you now have the financial freedom to achieve.

In addition, the questions help us determine whether you're a "toward motivator" or an "away motivator." A "toward motivator" is someone motivated to *do* things or *have* things that they don't currently have. An "away motivator" is predominantly motivated to *stop* doing things or *escape* from things they are now doing. Hence, a "toward motivator" is spurred by a desire to achieve something – a scuba diving vacation at one of the world's great coral reefs – whereas an "away motivator" is motivated by a desire to quit a job she doesn't like. In the general population, about 60 percent of us are primarily "away motivators" while 40 percent are "toward motivators."

For me, it's important to identify these two personality types because, for example, when "away motivators" plan for retirement, their overriding motivation is usually to *stop* working. They're energised by the thought that they will someday stop doing this or that. If I didn't know what motivated them, I might focus on what they wanted to achieve. For an "away motivator," that can be a conversation killer. Therefore, I do my best to lock into their mindset and direct the conversation towards subjects that inspire and excite them.

Many entrepreneurs are "toward motivators," so if I open a conversation with, "What are the things in your life you'd like to get rid of?" they'll likely say, "I haven't got any." This doesn't mean there aren't things they dislike; it's just that the desire to *escape* from something doesn't excite them. "Toward motivators" are accomplishment-focused people.

Record Your Goals

What doesn't get recorded often doesn't happen. If it's part of your plan, it must be documented. In addition, this makes the goals available to your Financial Planner for periodic reviews/updates. The first thing we do during progress appraisal meetings is review clients' progress towards their goals to ensure they are still relevant, and that their recent activities have aligned with achieving them.

It's perfectly fine to start the planning process with no goals or objectives. It's not uncommon for people to develop these as they go along. Fact is, most people do *not* have specific goals at the beginning of the process – at least none that can be measured or monitored.

Is retirement a goal? Yes, but it's an extremely vague goal – not the sort we want for you. The types of goals we want to see should fit SMART criteria – they must be Specific, Measurable, Attainable, Realistic and Timely. Although "retirement" may have a date assigned to it, and is usually realistic and attainable, it is extremely unspecific and, therefore, difficult to measure in a meaningful way – in terms of achieving a particular lifestyle through a certain level of income. SMART goals should be written in the present tense; it's mentally easier if we tell ourselves our goals have already happened. For example, "It is now 2019 and I have £50,000 available to help fund my three grandchildren through their university education."

When people first come to us, most don't have specific goals. If they do, they often represent incremental enhancements of their current routines and lifestyles. "I want a bit more of this and a bit less of that." In the beginning, people tend to think small. They allow inertia to carry them along the same path they've been following for 30 or 40 years rather than considering new paths – volunteer work, second careers, new homes, new hobbies. What we suggest is that you at least *consider* some truly breakthrough ideas.

Of course, not everyone is interested in designing a new lifestyle or testing breakthrough ideas, and that's fine. It doesn't hurt to discuss such changes, but it's not the job of a Financial Planner to force these changes on you. In my opinion, however, it *is* the job of a Financial Planner to at least *suggest* the possibilities and opportunities that are open to you. From there, the rest is up to you. Some people will never examine new possibilities; others will leap at the chance. And still others will need time before they gradually implement some of the suggestions.

People rarely move quickly from one extreme to another. Some will, but most people prefer to take "baby steps." My job isn't to force you to explore new possibilities, but to make you aware of the possibilities and let *you* decide what to do from there.

Case in point: One of my clients is a childless retired couple in their mid-60s with assets of approximately £400,000. Of that, half is in a house and half in an investment portfolio. However, their pension income pays all the bills. At a recent meeting I said to them, "I've done an analysis, and can demonstrate that even if you need to go into a care home, the money in the house will largely pay for all of that. Given this, why not do something now with the remaining £200,000? Why not enjoy life a little more, while your health's okay and you can do more things? The analysis indicates that even if you went on a massive spending binge over the next 10 years, you wouldn't run out of money."

I thought to myself, "They won't go on a massive binge, but this should be enough to get them kick-started."

When I visited them six months later, I beheld the fruits of the "massive spending binge." The husband had purchased a new television – for less than £300. It wasn't very big; he could have gone to the local Tesco, tucked the thing under his arm, and walked out with it.

"Okay, *that* approach didn't work," I thought, so I tried a different tack. Noting that a good opportunity had arisen to make a withdrawal from their investment fund, I said, "What I want to do is pay you £10,000, and because the two of you can't agree on what to do with the money, I'll give you £5,000 apiece. Just spend this £5,000. You can spend it over the next six months or twelve months or you can spend it in one go. Just go and spend it. Enjoy it."

His wife wanted to use the money to travel, while the husband decided to spend it on an engineering project (he's a retired engineer). Eventually, this approach did the trick. They finally began to spend a substantial amount of their surplus income. They still haven't spent all of it, but they've spent more than £300 on a TV. This situation is representative of how many people, slowly and incrementally, make changes to their lifestyles and begin realising some of their dreams once their Financial Planner shows them what it is possible to do with their money.

As you develop your goals, write them down. Create a record. And make sure the goals and visions are SMART. Frequently, this requires extensive discussions with your spouse, your family members, and your Financial Planner. However you come to develop them, record and structure your goals so they can be referenced again and again.

3A. Identifying Opportunities, Threats and Resources

You can find this tool online:

thefamilylegacysolution.co.uk/your-vision

4. Family Impact Discussions

AFTER DEVELOPING A KEEN UNDERSTANDING of your financial resources and commitments during the Capability Explorer phase, and distilling your objectives during the Vision Meeting, we combine these two discussions to construct a cohesive financial plan that we present during the Strategy Meeting. After that, we strongly recommend that you hold a Family Impact Discussion if needed. Not all financial plans or legacy plans have a family element to them – i.e. in cases where the family doesn't yet have sufficient funds to bequeath to other generations, or where they already have effective Wills, or where they don't have children and/or good causes as their principal beneficiaries.

The purpose of this meeting is to expand the conversation – to communicate the financial plan to affected family members and invite their questions and comments. This Family Impact Discussion also:

- Is a good time to make the next generation aware of the duties and responsibilities they will face if you become incapacitated and when you pass from the scene.
- Improves the chances that your wishes will be implemented after you're gone. If you don't speak with your heirs, and if your wishes and plans have not been recorded, there's much less chance of that happening.
- Enhances the financial awareness of children and grandchildren with regard to both the family's situation and their own circumstances.
- Can provide your heirs with methods to take control of their own finances.

This isn't to say, of course, that the meetings are never without challenges. Depending on the personalities involved and the family dynamics, you may confront headwinds. This is especially likely if your heirs have wildly different attitudes and approaches to money – if some children are high-earning professionals while others struggle to earn a living – or if there are strong sibling rivalries. Questions of fairness tend to arise within families that have undergone divorce and remarriage, or when too many heirs are present at the discussions. To keep such challenges from derailing the meeting, the person facilitating the meeting should create an agenda and stick to it. In addition, the facilitator should determine which topics are *not* to be discussed or divulged, though I recommend that you keep "forbidden" topics to a minimum.

I attend Family Impact discussions to offer counselling and, when necessary, provide technical guidance, but I don't lead them. That job belongs to the head(s) of the family. In my experience, these discussions are most productive when parents or grandparents run them. If need be, I can serve as an arbiter, but in general, parents and grandparents know best how to talk with their children.

As regards the meeting itself, it should be conducted at a mutually agreeable place – not necessarily the homes of parents or grandparents – that offers physical and psychological comfort for all participants, as well as access to refreshments. Set aside at least two or three hours with *no* possibility for interruptions. You might find it difficult to accomplish all of your goals for the meeting if someone's mobile phone keeps going off or if young children continually interrupt the discussions. I strongly recommend that you limit the list of invitees to children and grandchildren, and exclude spouses or partners of the children and grandchildren. If you decide to include spouses, then the list needs to include *all* spouses. If you invite only those spouses whom you like, for example, you may sow seeds of discontent and conflict for the future.

When it comes to preventing conflict among children, I tell clients that, unless their children are naïve and/or stupid, they probably have a good idea of what they stand to inherit. They may not know exactly how much, or the types of investments that have been made, but most children have a rough idea. As for sons- and daughters-in-law, they don't have to be part of the process. In many cases, it's a good idea to limit the dissemination of information to just the immediate family – your spouse and children. It's up to your children if they then want to share this information with spouses, but in my experience, it's best to limit *participation* in the actual planning process to spouses/partners and children.

In addition to excluding spouses/partners from the meeting, I recommend that they be excluded as beneficiaries and trustees. This protects the family's money in the event of divorce – unless, of course, you're so fond of your sons- and daughters-in-law that you *want* them to inherit assets, regardless of whether they stay married to your children. If spouses/partners demand to know why they've been excluded as heirs, it's best to say, "This is not about taking money away from you; this is about protecting money for the family bloodline and not the spouses or partners. It's not a criticism of you."

Because I have participated in many of these meetings, I've developed a sixth sense toward them. Today, I *know* in advance which meetings will succeed and which won't. I've found that when I have the chance to talk with heirs in advance, or when the parents are very detail-oriented, that the Family Impact Discussion is more likely to accomplish all of their objectives.

Ideally, my clients will open the meetings by saying something such as, "Look, we have been working with a Financial Planner to determine what's important for our future. And we've decided to proactively develop our legacy within the family. In essence, that means we're thinking of doing *a*, *b* and *c*. We want to involve you in this process so you will know what that means when we die; what that means if we get sick; what that means if we need to go into a care home; and what that means if we give you some money today. We want to discuss with you what you would do with the money we bequeath you, and what difference that might make to you. Do you need income? Do you need capital? How could we best do that?"

I think your Financial Planner should be present at these meetings, but that he or she should not focus too much on solutions. Instead, the planner should serve as an adviser and counsellor, discussing – for example – what the duties and responsibilities of an executor are, or what it means to be a trustee.

At this stage, it's not important to delve into details about implementing the legacy solutions. That occurs later. What you can (and should) discuss now are the best options for funding things such as long-term nursing care for yourself, higher education for children and grandchildren, and planning and executing Wills and Trusts.

Funding Higher Education

With regard to higher education, the most important fact to recognize is that costs are rising. According to official figures, annual tuition fees now average £7,647. This means that the full cost of a three-year degree course averages £25,941. Although students from the poorest backgrounds may receive discounts and grants worth several thousand pounds, most undergraduates from middle-class families will probably be charged the full amount.[1] The cost of food and housing is also rising, along with the tuition fees.

Given these facts, it's important that families decide in advance how much, if anything, they plan to contribute to higher education. It's also important to realise that, in the U.K., a student can borrow the entire amount needed for tuition, food, and housing. Nobody is barred from going to a university. They are only barred, effectively, on the basis of whether they'll be able to pay back the loans within a reasonable timeframe and without undue hardship. Unfortunately, the financing costs of student loans are now higher than they used to be, so it's not as cost-effective for students to borrow heavily. Therefore, when you consider funding higher education, it's vital to analyse how this can be accomplished, and determine how many grandchildren you can assist. How many do you have today? Are you going to have more? What will the parents contribute? What will the child have to contribute? Who will benefit most from a university education? Is university a good option for a particular grandchild? (You don't want to finance someone's university education only to discover that he or she had a great time on campus but received no long-term benefits.) Also, how will you treat the grandchildren who aren't likely to need or want a higher education? Will they receive any financial assistance, or will they effectively be penalised because they've decided not to pursue an education that's unsuitable for them? Other issues to consider include:

☐ Do you want the beneficiaries to have control over the funds?

- When do you want to establish a saving account, Trust, or other investment strategy to help fund these educations? It could be Inheritance Tax-efficient for parents or grandparents to put money away now into Absolute Trust, but that could mean that children will receive that money at age 18, with no questions asked – even if they have no plans to attend university. Or do you put the money into a "Discretionary Trust" – a Trust in which there is no entitlement to either the capital or income?
- Do you want to hang on to the money to ensure that it's spent wisely on things that will truly benefit the beneficiaries? The issue here is, if you and your spouse pass away, the money may incur death duties, and you may still lose control over how it's spent.

These and other questions should be asked so that adequate planning can be undertaken. At The Family Legacy Solution, we typically establish funds for the specific purpose of funding higher education. There's no single investment product that is "perfect" for this end. It all depends on how much money you wish to devote for this purpose in relation to your overall financial situation, as well as your attitude toward Inheritance Tax. If tax isn't a special concern, it's probably best to retain control of the funds, investing them in separate pots and then doling out the money over time as needed.

Long-Term Care

In the U.K., long-term nursing care is primarily funded at the point of need, so there isn't a great deal that can be done in advance, especially as there are no longer investment products specifically designed to pay for this care. Such products may return at some point, but for now, our approach is to assume that care fees will rise faster than the rate of inflation and to advise our clients on this basis. Specifically, our advice depends on the options that our clients wish to choose or that they must choose. For example, will the care take place in the person's home or in a nursing home? Often, this isn't something you can control, but many people prefer to receive care in the home. If so, keep in mind that you'll need to continue paying your household bills. That said, nursing home care is often more expensive.

We commonly consider a long-term care annuity. At the point of need, the family arranges an annuity that exchanges the capital of the person going into care for income that pays for the care, effectively insuring the remainder of the assets for the family. The market is not well developed here in the U.K., but we tend to find that, depending upon the age and the health of the person in care, the *maximum* break-even point is about five years, and often much less. Without an annuity, the potential exists for an extended and costly stay in long-term care.

The father of one of my clients had a stroke, and was in a care home for nearly 10 years. Fortunately, the client had arranged a care annuity that was paid off after three years, and this protected all his father's assets. If he hadn't purchased the annuity, about £300,000 of his inheritance would have disappeared. (An annuity can provide security for the person in care with regard to their income and ability to meet the fees.)

Again, the risk of longevity is a big factor to consider. Although the average (or "mean") length of time that people spend in a care home is three years, the most common length of stay (or mode) is six months and five years.

Another point, with regard to long-term care, is the house: How do you view the equity in your house? The changes coming forward in this country have been prompted by the fact that it's politically unpalatable for people to go into care homes and have their houses taken from them to pay for the care. At the moment, the rules state that if one spouse goes into care, the value of the house is exempt from the care-fee analysis for means-testing. Effectively, if you have more than £23,000 of qualifying assets, you pay for *all* your care. If you have less than £16,000, the local authority pays for all of it.

It should be noted that transferring an asset out of your name does not necessarily mean that it will not be taken into account in a means test. The local authority can, when assessing a resident's eligibility for assistance, look for evidence of deliberate or intentional deprivation of capital such as a gift of property. Deliberate deprivation occurs when an individual transfers an asset out of his or her possession to put him or herself in a better position regarding the means test for care home accommodation (or to claim social security benefits)."[2]

If you enter a care home today, the local authority will perform the means test, and if they uncover any asset transfers that occurred within the previous six months, they can disqualify those transfers. If the financial manoeuvre was done *more* than six months ago, but the local authority determines that the transaction was conducted mainly for the purpose of depriving the person of assets for the means test, the local authority can still disallow the transfer.

CRAG (Charging for Residential Accommodation Guide) contains the rules used by local authorities for assessing means. One of the rules essentially states that if just one party goes into care, and either the spouse or the dependents still live in the house, the value of the house is exempt from the means-test calculation. The rule was put in place to ensure that relatively low-income people – those who own homes but little else in the way of investments – don't have their homes taken from them or have a charge placed on the home by the local authority to pay the costs of long-term nursing care. Unfortunately, if the first spouse were to die and then the second spouse entered care, the value of the house could be swallowed up because at this point nobody is commonly *living* in the house. In response, some people have given houses to their children, which probably won't solve the problem because, as I mentioned above, the local authority can simply undo the transaction. Even if such a transaction isn't disallowed, do you really want your future ex-son-in-law or ex-daughter-in-law to own part of your house? Given the current rates of separation and divorce, it's entirely possible that this could happen.

In sum, asset deprivation schemes rarely work.

A better route – one that's non-contestable – is to create an "immediate post-death interest" Trust. This gives the surviving spouse the right to an income from all assets of the first to die, including the right to stay in the home. The surviving spouse not only has the right to live in the home, but can also sell it, taking money out of the protection of the Trust. In other words, all assets, including the value of the first-to-die's share of the house, are exempt if the survivor needs long-term nursing care in the future.

Currently, the costs of long-term care are uncapped. If you live for 20 years, you pay for 20 years. If you live for three weeks, you pay for three weeks. During the first 12 weeks, your house is disregarded, but afterward, the local authority can take the house. They can take everything, if you have sufficient capital that precludes them from having to pay for your care. It appears likely, however, that the government will soon institute a lifetime cap of £72,000 against *medical* care costs. (Note: *medical* care costs do not include food and housing, which are termed "hotel costs.") Under the lifetime cap, once your medical bills have reached £72,000, the government will pay the rest. As of this writing, it has yet to be determined how much of a cap, if any, the government will place on hotel costs. The government has suggested a limit of £12,000 per annum, but the care home can charge more, so it's likely that patients and their families will remain on the hook for a lot of money.

Some Basics Facts about Wills

An alarming number of people believe it isn't necessary to draft a Will – if they intend to leave everything to a spouse or if the distribution of assets will be "simple," everything will flow to the beneficiaries by default. A 2010 survey by the Office of Fair Trading estimated that 53 percent of adults in England and Wales do not have a Will.[3]

In fact, it's *vital* to create a Will, regardless of the perceived value of your estate and the number of beneficiaries. If you die without a Will, the government will dictate how your money and property are allocated, and it's likely that some of these decisions won't be in accord with your wishes. (If you die intestate without a surviving spouse or relatives, the Crown gets everything.)

In order for a Will to be valid, it must be:
- In writing.
- Made by someone who is at least 18 years old.
- Made voluntarily and without pressure from another person.
- Made by someone who is of sound mind – i.e. you must be fully aware of the nature of the document being written and

- signed, as well as of the property being distributed and the identity of the beneficiaries.
- Signed by two witnesses in the presence of the person making the Will. *Note*: A witness or the married partner of a witness cannot benefit from the Will. If the witness is a beneficiary (or the married partner or civil partner of a beneficiary), the Will is valid, but the beneficiary will not be able to inherit under the Will.

Although it isn't necessary that a Will be drafted or witnessed by a solicitor, I strongly recommend that you retain one – if only to check the document for errors. It's easy, and quite common, for laypeople to make mistakes, and if there *are* errors in the Will, this could cause significant problems for beneficiaries. In a recent survey conducted by STEP (the Society of Trust and Estate Practitioners) 84 percent of STEP members said they had in the last year encountered at least one Will that contained drafting errors, and 60 percent had seen Wills with mistakes that could have invalidated them.[4] Among the most common mistakes:

- Failing to account for all of your assets.
- Choosing one or more beneficiaries who die before the Will is executed. In itself, this isn't a problem if the Will is worded correctly. For example, you can dictate who steps into whose shoes following the death of a beneficiary. It is not the selection of the beneficiaries that's a problem, but failing to create a contingency plan if one of your beneficiaries dies before you do. Of greater concern is deceased or incapable or inappropriate executors who need to be replaced.
- Failing to consider the effects that marriages, registered civil partnerships, divorces, or dissolutions of civil partnerships can have on a Will.
- Failing to account for rules that allow dependents to make claims on your estate if they believe they haven't been adequately provided for.

Even when you hire a solicitor to prepare the Will, it's a good idea to consider, in advance, the type of information you want to include. The task here is to list your assets to the solicitor and Financial Planner, as well as the beneficiaries and executors. (Note: unless you wish to bequeath a certain asset to a particular person, assets aren't normally mentioned in the Will.) Although you needn't appoint more than one executor, it's a good idea to do so – in case one of them dies or becomes incapacitated. It's common for people to appoint two executors, but any number can be named in a Will. However, only a maximum of four can actually undertake probate duties. Typically, people appoint relatives or friends as executors, as well as their solicitors, accountants, or banks.

Choose your executors with care, as the job comes with a great deal of work and responsibility. (If a potential beneficiary is a minor child, the responsibility of the executor could last for a number of years – until the child becomes an adult.) You should always approach anyone you are thinking of appointing to ensure that they want the responsibility. Failure to fulfil your wishes under the Will can make the executor personally liable to the beneficiaries. Some common mistakes made when appointing executors:

- ☐ Appointing someone who cannot be easily contacted.
- ☐ Appointing someone who is likely to die before you.
- ☐ Appointing joint executors who often disagree with each other.
- ☐ Appointing a person who is reluctant to undertake the job.
- ☐ Appointing someone who does not agree with your wishes.

If at any time you wish to make minor amendments to the Will, you can prepare a codicil. This supplement contains your minor alterations, but leaves the rest of the document intact. A codicil might be used, for example, to increase or decrease a cash legacy, to change an executor, or to add beneficiaries. There is no limit on the number of codicils that can be added to a Will, but they are suitable only for very straightforward changes. If complex changes are needed, it's best to make a new Will. The new Will should begin with a clause stating that it revokes all previous Wills and codicils, and the old Will should then be destroyed.

If you want to destroy a Will, you must burn it, shred it, or otherwise destroy it with the clear intention of revoking it, because there is a risk that if an earlier copy reappears (or parts of it are reassembled), it might be thought that the destruction was accidental. You must destroy the Will yourself or it must be destroyed in your presence. Please note that a simple instruction to an executor to destroy a Will has no effect.[56]

Transferring Values, Knowledge and Experience

There's more to a legacy than money and material possessions. Your legacy may also include the transfer of values, knowledge, skills, and experiences to succeeding generations. Transferring intangible assets, however, is not as simple as adding a codicil to your Will that contains a few business tips and life lessons. The values and wisdom you've acquired over the course of a lifetime are best transferred during the course of your life, especially when you lead by example. However, there are some "best practices" for transferring such information after you're gone. The father of one of my clients, for example, has decided to record his life story for the family in the form of a memoir. This could be a wonderful gift for the family, assuming he's able to finish the memoir before the ultimate deadline. Unfortunately, this seems increasingly unlikely. The father is in his late seventies and, at the moment, much of the information is still scattered across various journals. His opinion seems to be, "If I don't finish the work before I die, that's fine; the children can read the journals."

I doubt that.

In my experience, it's unlikely that children and grandchildren will make the effort to sift through assorted journals, notes, and other documents in search of nuggets of wisdom. They probably won't sit down to read all of this material unless it's available in their preferred media, whether print or digital, video or audio. Toward that end, we have begun videotaping interviews with some clients, so their heirs will have easy access to whatever information the client wishes to impart to the beneficiaries. Whether the recording is available on DVD, computer disc, or in the Cloud, it's important that it also be accessible. Written journals, memoirs, and autobiographies are fine if those are the favorite media of the beneficiaries, but it's my observation that the younger generation prefer electronic media over print. Audio recordings are acceptable, but I think video is much more powerful and immediate.

Charitable Giving

With regard to donating your time and money to worthwhile causes, there are several factors to consider, including *how much* time and money is available and how much you wish to give. It's my experience that charitable giving works best when you combine time with money – if only because this gives you more control over how the funds are spent.

At one extreme, you can set up a charitable Trust. You can fund the Trust while you're alive and/or after you pass on, and you can either use the funds in the charitable Trust yourself – effectively registering it as a separate charity – or use the money to fund contributions to other charities. Realistically, this approach requires a couple of hundred thousand pounds, if it is to be funded while you're alive, to make it worthwhile. The chief benefit is, of course, that you can exercise a great deal of control over the disbursement of the money, whether you decide to turn the Trust into a full-time job for yourself or to merely write some checks and be done with it.

A less ambitious but no less worthwhile approach is to look for charitable giving opportunities at the local level. Donating to local causes – to organisations located close to where you live – can allow you to make a bigger impact for a smaller amount of money, with the added benefit of actually witnessing the results of your efforts.

If you decide to leave money in your Will, it's important to make the bequests as fixed sums rather than *percentages of the net estate*, because you can't know what the total value of the estate will be upon your death, given the impacts of inflation, long-term care fees, and other factors. (The trick is to leave monetary amounts for charities that won't create problems for the executors, and to periodically review those amounts.) Charities entitled to percentages of an estate can be a nightmare for executors, as they will want evidence that the funds they receive are the true amounts due to them. Therefore, we often suggest fixed monetary amounts and review these on a regular basis to ensure the amounts remain appropriate. (This does not apply if you are leaving the funds to your own charitable Trust.)

Regardless of the good deeds done by charitable organisations, some are rather ruthless when it comes to claiming money bequeathed to them. If, for example, you decide to leave 10 percent of your estate to an organisation, but the total value of the estate shrinks from £1,000,000 to £100,000 by the time you pass on, it's likely that your family will be the ones to suffer. The charity and its legal representatives will ensure that it receives every penny to which it's entitled under the Will.

That aside, another reason to leave money to charities is the tax relief available to those who make charitable bequests in their Wills.

Currently, if the value of your estate exceeds £325,000, Inheritance Tax will be levied at a rate of 40 percent on any assets above that threshold. (It's also charged on gifts made less than seven years before your death.) As property prices have risen, Inheritance Tax has become a reality for more and more people. Today, it isn't uncommon for the value of a home to push someone's estate over the threshold. However, if you leave money to a qualifying charity, or give money to that organisation within seven years prior to your death, it will not be assessed as part of your estate for Inheritance Tax purposes. This is a popular means by which Inheritance Tax bills can be reduced or avoided while ensuring that favourite causes benefit from your largesse. Also if the charitable gift is greater than 10 percent of the taxable estate (i.e. the amount over the threshold), then the tax paid on the balance falls by 10 percent (to 36 percent). Smart calculations can often provide a meaningful charitable bequest at little or no cost to the other beneficiaries (the family).

Lifetime Gifts

How much would you like to bequeath to beneficiaries – now and after you die?

How old will your beneficiaries be if you wait until you die to transfer some of your assets: 55, 65 or 75? Do you really want to transfer wealth to your children at the *end* of their careers? Why not arrange to make *lifetime gifts* to your children and grandchildren?

Not everyone is able to make substantial lifetime gifts. Sometimes the arithmetic reveals that there aren't enough surplus resources (capital or income). Therefore, one of the first things your Financial Planner should do is determine how much surplus capital or income you have and what you can afford to give.

I'm a big advocate of lifetime giving, as long as the numbers add up and the heirs will benefit from the gifts. In addition to seeing the money used and enjoyed while you're alive, the biggest benefit of lifetime giving is being able to exercise control over when the funds are disbursed and how the money is spent (or *not* spent).

To ensure that your heirs receive the maximum benefit from lifetime gifts, it's best to create a programme in tandem with your Financial Planner. The programme will determine how much money will be given away over a certain period of time, and will also target how the funds will be used. Be sure to engage in conversations with your family before committing to these objectives. Remember, a legacy plan is based on conversations with the family, the beneficiaries, on how and when assets should be distributed. Engage with your family members. Talk with them about how the money should be used. Also keep in mind the likely consequences of these gifts – if you give the money to your children to pay off their mortgages, what are they going to do with the extra monthly income this allows them? Are they going to spend it going down the pub or going on holiday, or are they going to do something that *you* might consider more useful?

You might want to employ a discretionary Trust arrangement for substantial gifts. By giving someone a cheque, even if you believe they'll do something useful with the money, you lose total control over what happens next. Typically, people put funds for minor children into what's called a "bare Trust." Under this arrangement, children receive that money outright when they're 18 so, effectively, you lose control at that point. Under a discretionary Trust, the beneficiaries have no right to income or capital. While you're alive, you act as a trustee, controlling where the money goes. When you're gone, normally the next generation would take over the trusteeship.

To retain some control, however, you can prepare a letter of wishes – one that states where you want the money to go. This doesn't guarantee that the funds will go precisely where you want them, but it will afford you protection from the potential impacts of divorce, spendthrift beneficiaries, bankruptcy, or children dying before their spouses and leaving everything to them. In general, if the money is still being held in trust, this keeps your assets out of the estates of the beneficiaries, so when the beneficiaries die, the money is not in *their* estates. This can provide significant tax benefits to your descendants while allowing them to continue reaping the benefits of the money in your estate.

Your trustees have three options when it comes to handling the money remaining in that Trust. One is to transfer out, to do away with the Trust. This is a good option if the rules governing Trusts change in the future. (Also, here in the U.K., there is a law against perpetuities, meaning a Trust can operate only for 125 years before it has to be terminated.)

Another option is to invest the Trust funds in the Trust, which allows them to defer decisions on how/when money is spent by the beneficiaries. The downside is that income and capital gains on investments in the Trust are invariably subject to high tax rates.

The third and final option, one that we favour when beneficiaries have proven themselves to be responsible adults, is to make interest-free loans from the Trust. Because the loans are interest free, there is no tax on the capital gains, but the beneficiaries receive the same amounts as if you'd just written them a cheque. When the generation that received the loans dies, the money is paid back into the Trust from their estates. Yes, the value of the money has been eroded by inflation but in the interim, the Trust has probably been protected from potential depredations by the previous generation.

This approach is known as a Beneficiary Protection Trust, which is set up during your lifetime. It allows both lifetime gifts and bequests to be routed through the Trust. In addition to providing funds to the children now, the Beneficiary Protection Trust provides the opportunity for the rules that govern it to be those that existed when it was created, rather than those that may exist in the future (which could be less advantageous). These Trusts are living entities. To register at the outset, we put a £10-note on each of them, which means that the settlors can put money into the Trusts while they're alive. Then, when the person dies, the remainder of their estate (post-tax, post-expenses, post-debt repayment) goes into these Trusts. We can use these Trusts to accomplish all kinds of tangible benefits, from providing money to help children and grandchildren pay off their mortgages to putting children through school or placing deposits on new homes.

Another approach to lifetime giving involves gifts that qualify for Inheritance Tax exemptions. Even if the value of your estate exceeds the threshold, you can sometimes transfer assets without paying Inheritance Tax. For example, there is usually no Inheritance Tax to pay on anything you leave to a spouse or civil partner, including gifts made while you're alive. Also, if you live for seven years after making a gift to someone, it's exempt from Inheritance Tax regardless of its value. (*Note*: if you continue to benefit from something you've given, it **will not** be exempt. This is known as a "gift with reservation of benefit." For example, if you give away your house but continue to live in it without paying the market rate of rent, the "gift" will not be exempt.)

In addition, you can give away up to £3,000 a year, and the money will be exempt from Inheritance Tax when you die. You can also make small gifts – up to £250 – to as many people as you like (though you cannot add this amount to the £3,000 annual exemption for the same person).

Wedding and civil partnership gifts are also exempt, within limits. Each parent of the couple can give cash or gifts worth up to £5,000, while grandparents can each give up to £2,500, and everyone else can give up to £1,000. (*Note*: you must make the gift on or before the date of the wedding or civil partnership ceremony.)

If you own or share a business, you may be able to pass some of it on without paying tax, and the same holds true if you own a working farm. If you have woodland, the value of the timber (but not the land) is excluded from your estate. In addition, if you own something of historic or scientific interest, it could be exempt from Inheritance Tax. Examples include buildings of outstanding historic or architectural interest, as well as objects with national scientific, historic, or artistic interest. However, these assets have to be made available for the public to view.[7]

Be sure to keep record of these gifts, especially those that might be subject to Inheritance Tax if you exceed certain thresholds (or where exemption requires that seven years pass between the date of the gift and your death.)

Another thing to bear in mind: when doing calculations for Inheritance Tax, *always take into account future asset appreciation*. It's all well and good to do a calculation now, thinking, "If I die tomorrow, the tax man's going to get £100K," but at the moment, the Inheritance Tax nil-rate band of £325,000 is set to remain fixed until 2017-18. *According to recent research by the Institute for Fiscal Studies, the proportion of estates liable for Inheritance Tax will quadruple from just 2.6 percent in the 2009-10 tax year to 10 percent in 2018-19.*[8]

That being said, don't allow the "tax-saving tail" to wag the "lifetime-giving" dog. There are some structures (predominantly Trust structures) that can be used to tick off many tax-saving boxes, but they're often little more than marketing gimmicks, in my opinion. Suffice it to say that many complex investment and tax-saving schemes are very appealing on face value, but after some simple analysis with your Financial Planner, you'll likely discover that most aren't suitable for your long-term needs and goals.

5. Implementing Your Financial Plan

ONCE THE FINANCIAL PLAN HAS BEEN CREATED, it's time to activate it. From this point forward, the benefits of the plan – one that includes every detail of your investment strategy – become abundantly clear. It now serves as a blueprint and a point of reference that holds you, your Financial Planner, and any other advisers accountable for future decisions. For example, if you delegate all or part of the investment management process to a financial adviser, you could hand him the document and say, "This is what I'm trying to achieve. I want you to do *this*." The plan is also important for review purposes, allowing you to later evaluate your progress against the timescales and other benchmarks you established at the outset. While there's no such thing as a "representative" strategy meeting – one that exemplifies how the process works for every family in every instance – the meetings usually adhere to the following agenda:

- ☐ We open the meeting by reiterating your objectives.
- ☐ From there, we summarise the main assumptions that we've made about earnings, inflation, rates of return, LTC fees, etc.
- ☐ We then present our top-down conclusions. ("Can you do all of this? If not, how far can you go?")
- ☐ Next, we project your income, expenditures, and net worth for the rest of your life, presenting your additional expenditure commitments in the form of graphics *and* numbers.
- ☐ We then recommend ways to achieve the objectives, addressing each area in turn – focusing first upon your immediate needs (repaying debt, savings, contingencies, insurances, etc.) before discussing legacy planning, longer-term investments, pensions, and so forth.

- ☐ Next, we provide you with a summary of what you need to do and when. We don't go into a lot of specifics at this stage. We can provide details after the strategy meeting and, if your concerns are product-related, during the following implementation phase.
- ☐ Finally, we present you with an action plan arranged in chronological order.

The chief benefit of a written plan is providing you with a quantifiable way to review and evaluate the entire strategy, ensuring that no one inadvertently "moves the goalposts" during the implementation phase. If you *do* decide to change your goals and strategies, a good Financial Planner will refer back to the plan, asking pointed questions about why you want to deviate from the roadmap. On a number of occasions, referencing the plan and asking, "Are you *sure* you want to do that?" has helped me prevent clients from succumbing to irrational exuberance.

Common Obstacles to Implementation

This isn't to say that the road to implementation is always free of bumps and potholes. Several common obstacles may interfere with the smooth execution of the plan. These include:

Analysis Paralysis: Overwhelmed by the need to act, some people are gripped by indecision. In their minds, there are too many things to do, to evaluate, to review and re-evaluate before they can put the plan into effect. Often, the people affected by this analysis paralysis are perfectionists. They continually fret that something's been left out of the plan, that something needs to be included, or that something needs to be revised before it's ready to implement (which date may never come if the person is allowed to procrastinate indefinitely). Rest assured that a good Financial Planner will be very thorough in his planning. He won't exclude information because he didn't think it was important – it's *all* important – and he won't be satisfied with a slap-dash approach to the process. At some point, however, you must take action. One of the worst things you can do is to get bogged down by the minutiae and/or some vague notion of what "perfection" feels like.

Here's a classic example of analysis paralysis.

ME: "Mr. X, you need to change your Will. If you don't, it's possible that *a*, *b* and *c* will occur after your death, which are all contrary to your wishes."

MR. X: "Yeah, yeah, I understand."

ME: "You'll need to include this and that information, and then follow these steps."

MR. X: "Yeah, I get it."

ME: "We'll also need to appoint executors and trustees."

MR. X: "Who shall I appoint?"

ME: "In this case, you might not want to appoint your children, because they're too young [or they don't get along or they live too far away].

MR. X: "So, who should I appoint?"

ME: "Just appoint *someone* and, in six months' time, you can go back and change it, if necessary, for very little money. It's better to choose *someone* today, and put everything in order, than to procrastinate."

MR. X: "So, who should I appoint?"

Six months later, Mr. X still hasn't appointed trustees or executors, because he wants to choose the "perfect" person or persons.

Yes, it's important to choose wisely when it comes to trustees and executors, but there comes a time when you simply have to say, "I *have* to get this done. Absent perfection, I need to settle for good enough."

Cost-consciousness: Just as they approach the threshold to implementation, some people balk at the costs. Just as the time arrives to "pull the trigger" following all of the hard work, they say, "Hold on! I've got to pay for this? I've got to pay for that?"

Some people choose *this* juncture to start haggling with planners over fees and expenses, despite the fact that every good planner will have fully disclosed all of the costs at the very start of the process. In other instances, cost-conscious clients open up the "Do-it-yourself-investment box" and become overwhelmed by the myriad options that might save a little money. To this, we always say, "We don't care if you buy and manage investments yourself. We're not trying to generate investment sales. We *have* investment solutions, and we can provide you with some if you need them, but we'll give you sufficient information to make those investments yourself if you'd like."

The moment some people open the DIY-investment box, they are trapped in an endless cycle of procrastination. On the one hand, they're now determined to save some money by investing for themselves. On the other, they're frequently unable to actually make investments because they're afraid of making mistakes or they become overwhelmed by the sheer number of options. This is the same mindset that spawns "buyer's remorse." It's the hallmark of the sort of person who's never satisfied with what he's ordered in a restaurant because, whatever he chooses, he later decides that it didn't taste as good as what he *could* have chosen. "The steak was lovely, but I should have ordered the fish! Why didn't I order the fish!?"

Research indicates that when people are presented with too many choices, they're less likely to make a decision. For that reason, one benefit of working with a Financial Planner is leadership – the leadership required to present and defend specific *recommendations.*

At The Family Legacy Solution, we review the alternatives, but we also guide clients towards the best choices. This helps them take timely action while avoiding buyer's remorse.

We don't simply say, "We've looked at your situation and come up with five options. Here are the pros and cons of all five. Take your pick."

Instead, we might say, "Here are five options and the pros and cons of all five. However, *this* is the one we recommend and why."

Sometimes clients don't need to know about options two, three, four, and five, because these aren't good choices. Ultimately, clients pay us to *advise* them, not to confuse them with undifferentiated options. We might tell someone that we discounted this or that option for x and y reasons, and they're free to override our recommendations, but we know that if we gave everyone too many choices, they might never reach a decision.

A Structured Process

We structure the implementation phase according to a timetable, breaking down the process into discrete and manageable steps. Thanks to this, clients always know what to do next, as well as when and with whom. At the very outset, we ask, "How do you want to proceed? We can go full-speed with every component of the plan, or we can implement components one at a time."

Some people don't want to take on too many tasks at once. They would rather handle one at a time, and that's fine. However, this doesn't mean that I will allow someone to dawdle. Once the process begins, I can be very persistent at keeping people on track. "You need to do this. Please do it. We're here to help, so let's do it." Although I expect clients to be proactive, this doesn't mean that I will go away if they are *not* proactive. Inactivity is counterproductive, so if you disappear for too long, I will start "nagging" you. Financial and legacy planning is a long process; it can take months, if not years, to move through every phase. If I left everyone to their own devices, some tasks would never get done. Everyday life has a way of distracting people from medium-term and long-term objectives. One of the jobs of the Financial Planner is to ensure that you stay on task. The moment we disappear is the moment everyday concerns will start overtaking clients again.

In addition, it's important to make sure that the entire family stays involved to some degree – beyond the Family Impact Discussion. Particularly when it comes to Wills, Trusts, and gifting, it's important to *keep* children involved. This is also another way to ensure that parents stay on track – by having someone other than the planner reminding them of what needs to be done.

At The Family Legacy Solution, the implementation process is structured, but it's also flexible. There are no fixed deadlines by which activities must be accomplished. Rather, the process resembles a menu of activities that must be addressed in the order of their priority. We help clients prioritise what needs to be done first, second, third, and then develop a schedule based on this information. The schedule is also based on our evaluation of each person's preferences for how and when to accomplish tasks – one task at a time, everything at once, or by another schedule.

Please note, however, that our first priorities are almost always the "what if" disaster scenarios that might occur in your life and how to deal with them – death, sickness, unemployment, or disability. By addressing these "what if" situations first, we can set up the requisite insurance policies, Wills, and cash flows to protect you from these unexpected events. For obvious reasons, we want to do this before addressing less urgent matters such as savings, pensions, and investment portfolios. Otherwise, we are normally quite flexible in terms of establishing and implementing priorities.

6. Choosing an Investment Strategy

WILL YOU *NEED* A COMPREHENSIVE investment strategy? If your primary financial objective is access to capital, rather than a return on your assets – ensuring that you will have sufficient funds to meet known future expenditures and contingencies – the answer may be "no." If, however, your goals extend beyond the fulfillment of short-term needs and contingencies, and you care about the performance of your assets, the answer is almost certainly "yes." The difference between these two strategies highlights the distinction between saving and investing, which is one of the most common topics I discuss with clients.

Saving versus Investing

Every individual with accessible capital needs to be aware of this distinction, because a failure to properly consider the differences between saving and investing can lead to major disappointment.

Savings are assets intended for use in meeting known expenditures in the short-term or unknown future expenditures (contingencies). With savings, the main concern is usually access to funds and the security of capital, rather than the potential for return on that capital. By contrast, investments are assets that are put to use for other longer-term purposes. Rather than access to funds or capital security, a return on the capital is the priority. Only when savings requirements have been met can you move on to consider investments. The two most common mistakes here are:
1. Using investments to fund savings requirements. If this is done, the value of the investment might fall just before the funds are needed, giving rise to disappointment ... or worse.

2. Holding excessive assets in liquid form (e.g., bank deposits) when all conceivable saving needs have already been met. In this instance, the investment return over time is likely to be mediocre, often failing to keep pace with inflation. Such an approach may significantly reduce the real value of the family's net worth, so excess funds should always be committed to an investment strategy.

When attempting to quantify your savings requirements, consider the following:

- *Known future capital expenditures* – usually those that will arise within the next three years. Some examples are a new car, home improvements, or education costs.
- *An allowance* to meet expected shortfalls in regular income against regular expenditures. Having two to three years' of income requirement in savings is very prudent.
- *Contingency fund*. This is a source of funds held solely to meet unforeseen expenditures. Quantifying the need for a contingency fund is something that must be done on a case-by-case basis. Frequently, the greatest determining factor is a personal preference about the size of the funds. Other considerations should be the security of your income in various "what if" scenarios – unemployment, sickness, disability – and how the income would compare against core expenditures (those that cannot be easily reduced). In such cases, a fund equal to at least six months (and preferably twelve months) of expenditures should be held.

Helping you navigate the savings versus investments decision is a key role of any Financial Planner. A thorough budget analysis can highlight the need for both contingency funds and any income needs.

What Is Investment Risk?

Central to every discussion I have with my clients about creating or reviewing their investment strategies is the concept of risk. One of my biggest challenges, however, is gaining a complete understanding of what *clients* mean by "risk" and how it relates to them. One person's views about risk will be very different from another's.

What are the common risks associated with any investment strategy? In many cases, the first point of discussion is the potential for capital value to decrease. People tend to associate the potential for capital losses with "riskiness." While it would be nice to think of risk in such simple terms, doing so can be dangerous.

First, potential loss of capital is only one measure of risk. A time factor also must be considered. Although some investments should never fall in nominal value – e.g., a bank account – others, such as a portfolio of shares, are often subject to capital loss. Statistics show, however, that if you extend the holding period for such a portfolio, the likelihood of facing an absolute capital loss decreases. In other words, your portfolio of shares is more likely to lose money over one week than over the course of a year or a decade. In sum, the risk of capital loss tends to decrease as the period of ownership increases. Risk can also encompass:

- The impact of short- to medium-term variations in income, rather than capital.
- The risk that invested proceeds will purchase fewer goods and services at the projected end of the strategy than if the money were spent today – the risk that returns will not keep pace with inflation.
- The risk that the underlying portfolio will not keep pace with your periodic withdrawals, thereby leading to capital erosion.
- The risk of investing too much money in one basket (stock, fund or sector risk), no matter how attractive that may seem.
- The risk of relying too heavily on U.K.-centric investments, thereby losing out on those available overseas. (However, currency exchange rate risk must be considered.)
- The risk that your vision or goals will change significantly, resulting in an investment strategy that isn't flexible enough to be updated accordingly.
- The risk that tax rules or legislation may change, negatively affecting your returns.

This list is by no means exhaustive, but it gives you an idea of the many dimensions that accompany investment strategy risks. I spend a great deal of time reviewing risks to clients' strategies – and for good reason. My experience shows that disappointment with investments usually arises when the underlying investments do not match the clients' perceived tolerance towards risk.

It is critical to review some (or more) of these concepts on a regular basis. Although it may be tempting to use what I call a "tick box" approach to risk appraisal, without undertaking in-depth discussions, I firmly believe that it's time well spent to effectively consider what degree of risk can *and cannot* be maintained within an investment strategy.

Assessing Your Risk Tolerance

Before advising you about strategies and recommending specific investment products, a Financial Planner should thoroughly assess your risk tolerance to achieve the proper balance between your wish for capital growth/income and the competing desire for security. Make no mistake: this *always* requires a balancing act. Over the long term, it is impossible to achieve high returns *and* low volatility. The most aggressive investments always carry higher volatility, while the safest are always the least profitable. The "trick," therefore, is finding each client's "sweet spot" – the zone in which the investor comfortably achieves goals while minimising the risk of losses.

At The Family Legacy Solution, we begin our risk tolerance assessment using the questionnaire at the end of this chapter. More subjective but just as valuable, we also query clients on their attitudes towards risk by posing hypothetical scenarios and asking them how they'd respond in these situations. From there, we develop a risk tolerance score, which is a number from 1 to 10, with 1 being someone with almost no tolerance for losses and 10 being someone with an extremely high tolerance. If we are working with a married couple, we complete a risk profile assessment for both husband and wife. We also prepare separate risk assessment profiles for each investment pot – one for retirement, one to fund education fees, one for a Trust fund, etc.

The questionnaire and hypothetical questions are a launchpad for more detailed conversations we will have with you. After all, a single-digit numeral doesn't tell us very much about how to design a bespoke investment strategy. It provides a good starting point, but we need to dig deeper. We need to discuss your capacity for loss on *specific* chunks of money devoted to specific objectives. This requires an understanding of three things:

1. *Your physical capacity for loss.* For example, if a particular sum were reduced by 50 percent or more during a particular timeframe, what would be the physical impact on your standard of living? In some respects, we coach you like we would a gambler in a casino to ensure that you don't risk money you can't afford to lose. Our job is to avoid exposing you to unacceptable degrees of risk – and to prevent you from doing it.
2. *Your emotional capacity for loss.* Even if you could afford to lose the money, how would this affect you emotionally? The worst case scenario is that, when temporary losses are experienced, you panic. You can't stand the pressure, so you sell at the bottom of the market and never recover the original investment. I've seen this happen many times, especially when a client's previous adviser misdiagnosed the risk tolerance. It then became *my* job to keep my wits about me while all around me were losing theirs and blaming it on me.

I usually say to panicked people, "Unfortunately, the worst-end-case scenario has happened for you right at the start. But investments always come back. We just don't know how long it's going to take. It might go down further before it turns around. The worst thing you can do now is to liquidate your position in a declining market. Do you understand?"

"Yes."

The client calms down.

A month later, I receive a phone call. The investment is now down by a further 10 percent, which requires me to give the person the same pep talk. And then another month passes, and I receive another phone call because the investment has dropped by 20 percent again. I try my best to talk people through these difficult times, but inevitably, the day will come when I receive an email telling me to liquidate the investment. I do it, but I also follow up with a phone call, saying, "Please make sure that you never invest in anything like this again. In three years' time, when this investment has returned to profitability, don't get greedy and put your money back into such investments again. It's not for you."

> 3. *Your investment experience.* How much investment experience and knowledge do you have? How have you actually responded to losses (if any) that you've experienced in the past? Often, the portrait that emerges from this discussion is more revealing than what we learn from any other conversation.

Throughout the whole risk assessment process – from filling out questionnaires to discussing your risk tolerance (physical, emotional and historical), it is vital that you be scrupulously honest with yourself and your Financial Planner. These evaluations will have a profound impact on the strategies that we recommend on your behalf.

Unfortunately, two major risks will always remain, and every investor has to decide how they want to balance their investments vis-à-vis these risks, because you cannot eliminate both. The risks are: (1) short-term volatility, the risk that your investments might go down in the short-term, which is probably what most people understand by investment risk; and (2) inflation – that when it's time to withdraw your money, it won't buy as much as it did when you made the investment. Eliminating one risk means accepting more of the other. Regardless of what a salesman might say, there is no single investment that provides capital security *and* inflation protection, which is why it's important to develop an accurate risk tolerance score for every investor. In terms of the 1-10 risk tolerance scale, someone who ranks a 1 is totally concerned with mitigating short-term volatility risk, while someone who is a 10 is totally concerned with inflation risk. Someone who is 5 or 6 is midway between the two risks.

Another point: risk tolerance assessments are designed to identify risks that you are *confident* about taking, not necessarily the risks that you *need* to take to achieve your objectives. That requires a separate conversation. If we perform a cash-flow analysis and determine that you're likely to have a surplus, you're now faced with three choices: (1) you can do nothing; (2) you can spend or gift the additional money; or

(3) you can take less risk with the overall investment strategy. If you choose the third option, this may provide a more comfortable "ride." You can expect lower returns, but this is a trade-off that some people are willing to make in exchange for reduced volatility and greater peace of mind. This option is also something that people frequently overlook. You may be *comfortable* being a number 7 on the risk tolerance scale, but do you really *need* to take that much risk when you can achieve the same objectives as a number 3?

Conversely, some people may need to increase their risk or scale back their objectives. Following a cash analysis we might say, "Though you would like to be a number 4 on the scale, this would require you to reduce your objectives, increase the timescale, or invest more money, which is fine. However, you *could* also take more risk. This approach isn't guaranteed to pay off, but we want you to know that you have the option. Just because you were initially identified as this or that number on the risk tolerance scale doesn't mean that you are locked in to that level of risk."

The level of risk with which someone feels comfortable is often higher than the level of risk they *need* to take, but unfortunately, that's not always the case.

It's impossible to quantify with certainty how much risk someone will actually feel comfortable taking. Some people make mistakes, thinking they'll be comfortable as a 7 when they are really more comfortable as a 2 or 3.

Regardless of your emotional risk tolerance, you must always be cognisant of the savings/investment distinction. As we saw during the recent economic downturn, some people lost money they could ill afford to lose because they unwisely *invested* their savings in volatile products. Essentially, these people gambled with funds that they should have earmarked for low- or no-risk accounts. Never invest money that you'll need for known expenditures, especially short-term expenditures, in products designed for long-term growth, no matter what your emotional risk tolerance may be.

The Importance of Strategic Asset Allocation

Strategic Asset Allocation (SAA) establishes long-term asset allocation targets among different asset classes (stocks, bonds, etc.) based on your objectives, risk tolerance, and timetables. Over time, SAA is the most important determinant of the total return of a broadly diversified portfolio with limited market timing and other tactical influences. Studies support empirically the dominance of SAA in determining total return and return variability.[9]

In sum, SAA determines the percentages of your invested assets that will be put into stocks versus bonds versus real estate or other options. These percentages are maintained (approximately) over the course of the year through periodic rebalancing of the portfolio, which ensures that as certain asset classes grow in value faster than others, the portfolio isn't thrown "out of balance" or disproportionally weighted in favour of one asset class over another.

It's been said that up to 90 percent of returns are generated by making the right asset allocation decisions – from choosing the right assets and the right mixture of assets, particularly if the money is in passive investments relative to, say, fund manager decisions or tactical changes. In the short term, other factors come into play. Some fund managers may outperform market indexes, which will add more value to the portfolio, and these managers tend to believe that Tactical Asset Allocation (see below) or active fund management is more important than SAA. Over time, however, short-term gains tend to average out, thanks to funds and fund managers that underperform.

Over the long term, SAA is much more important in terms of added value, which is why my greatest focus is on making sure it's done correctly. It's not easy to explain the reasons in a book, but suffice it to say that factors like active fund management create far less value than well-constructed strategic asset allocations. This is one reason why The Family Legacy Solution doesn't primarily use active fund management – because of the time and resources needed to make it work. (Frankly, I don't think you *can* make it work consistently, but even if you could, the effort required to pick active fund managers, review them, and monitor them wouldn't justify the marginal benefits received.)

Tactical Asset Allocation Decisions

As opposed to SAA, which is a long-term strategy, Tactical Asset Allocation (TAA) tries to add value by shifting money to asset classes that are expected to over-perform (or shifting away from asset classes expected to under-perform) in the *short term*.

While creating an SAA, you and your Financial Planner might say, "Long-term, let's have *x* percent in bonds, *y* percent in equities, and *z* percent in cash equivalents." However, if at some point you and your planner form an opinion as to where the market is headed, you could implement a Tactical Asset Allocation to rearrange the split of your assets. So if the stock market crashes, you might say, "Let's put more in the stock market. Bonds are getting expensive, so let's allocate less to bonds." In other words, TAA is an active short-term strategy based on timing the market, whereas SAA is a more long-term passive approach to asset allocation.

Although it's useful to give yourself the flexibility to respond to changing market conditions, I do *not* recommend that you practice TAA very often, if at all. In many instances, TAA is overused, overrates the value of other asset classes and – if a great deal of active management takes place – unnecessarily adds to the cost of investing.

At The Family Legacy Solution, we do make tactical asset allocation decisions, but in a very limited way. We don't want you to be so passive about your portfolio that you leave everything alone despite momentous changes in the markets, but we also don't want you to engage in wild-eyed speculation. Regular automatic rebalancing should ensure that your portfolio is returned to its agreed asset allocation targets on a habitual basis, certainly once a year. That will do a lot of the work of TAA, because it forces you to buy low and sell high.

We discourage our managers from making lots of tweaks and big bets to passive investments – tweaks that may disrupt the Strategic Asset Allocation. We allow managers to make some decisions, but within a limited range of, say, plus or minus 10 percent around what the SAA should be. Hence, if the asset allocation split was 50 percent in equities, a manager could re-allocate up to 60 percent or go down to 40 percent, but couldn't go much beyond those targets.

TAA is great when the markets, on a long-term basis, are pretty crazy. It would have been very useful during the height of the tech boom if you decided to be underweight in stocks, or just before the financial crisis, when it would have been wise to sell certain asset types. At those times, exercising flexibility would have been the smart move. But more often than not, you'll want to stay close to your SAA targets.

K.I.S.S.

A key role of every Financial Planner is helping you navigate the complexity of various investment and tax solutions. A large number of options are available, many of which involve sophisticated approaches that are difficult for clients, and in many cases, difficult for advisers to comprehend. In my experience, financial planning works best when it's kept simple. The advice to **K.I.S.S.** (Keep It Simple, Stupid) should be followed more frequently. If a simpler solution is available – one that offers all, or nearly all, the benefits of a more complex alternative – you should have a very good reason before selecting a more complex option.

Some clients' situations are sufficiently complex to warrant a more bespoke solution, but in many cases an effective planning process will clear away most of the complexity and allow a simpler solution to be employed. Lazy or disorganised planning doesn't allow this, and can result in a more complex solution than what you actually need.

One example of a complex scheme used more often than necessary is the Discounted Gift Trust (DGT). Using a Trust tax structure and a suitable investment vehicle (often an investment bond) a DGT offers, on the face of it, a good way to achieve the following benefits:

- An annual "income" equal to five percent of the initial investment, payable until the death of the investor or until the fund is used up.
- Funds remaining upon death are available to the family. If death occurs more than seven years after the plan is created, such a payment will be free from Inheritance Tax.
- An immediate "discount" on the size of the investor's estate – i.e. part of the investment will not fall into the investor's

estate for IHT purposes, even if death occurs on the day after the investment is made.

Many clients, particularly those who have retired and have concerns about IHT, jump at the chance to acquire a relatively secure source of income and obtain (potentially tax-free) capital for the family. As a result, it's often an easy "sale" for an adviser, and one that attracts high initial fees and ongoing adviser charges, given the complexity of the plan and the need to monitor the capital investment to reduce the potential for capital erosion.

A little more work by the planner might cast a different light on the suitability of a DGT:

- Does the investor actually require an income? Although an extra source of income is always welcome, generating extra income in this case can be counterproductive. If the payments from the DGT are not used to meet the cost of living, they will simply accumulate within the investor's estate for IHT purposes, in effect nullifying over time the IHT benefits. A comprehensive budget planning approach might reveal that the additional income isn't needed.
- Is the investor aware of *all* the implications of the plan? Funds within a DGT cannot be accessed until the death of the investor. Therefore, if an investor lives much longer than expected, the family might not gain access to the funds for many years. Could the family better use the funds now, rather than much later?
- If the need for income is not great, do you require access to the capital? A cash flow analysis should be undertaken to determine the likelihood that you will need to access the capital in the proposed DGT investment.

My standard approach is to consider the current and projected financial resources of a client as: (A) resources they *will* need; (B) resources they *may* need; and (C) resources they *don't* need.

The question then becomes, where does a DGT fit within this analysis? If the investor will definitely need the funds to be invested, surely they would prefer full access to all the capital without tying it up in a Trust. If the investor may need the capital, it is likely to be of a lump sum nature, something that cannot be provided by a DGT. If the capital is not likely to be required, should the client not consider giving the funds away now, so the family can benefit immediately? When viewed in a simpler light, the short-term tax benefits of a DGT are often less attractive.

DGTs and other complex strategies *do* have their place, but the onus is on the planner to ensure that they are used only when necessary.

At The Family Legacy Solution, we believe that a Financial Planner's job is to remove complexity as much as possible. To accomplish this, we've established a process that helps us walk clients through the investment strategy process, one section at a time. We also provide scheduling, such that the client must (within reason) adhere to the process. Although we're happy to take the lead in crafting the overall strategy, the process doesn't have the same impact when clients aren't sufficiently involved in the process, both emotionally and physically.

Matching Assets to Objectives

Although it's important to consider risk tolerance and your age when choosing investments, these factors shouldn't be your main (or only) selection criteria. Instead, choose investments that match your specific objectives and timescales. At the start of the process, ask yourself, "What are my objectives? How much will these objectives cost to achieve? What needs to be invested now – and what needs to be invested between now and when the funds are needed – to achieve the goals?" Create a separate investment pot, strategy, and process for each objective, and then tie them all together under the umbrella of your overall investment strategy and process.

For young people – those who are comfortable taking risks, and with retirement still decades away – taking a fair degree of volatility risk may be suitable. However, some clients in their twenties and thirties want to use their ISAs to help purchase, say, a house in three or five years. Here, they need to be more cautious. Many investors fall into the trap of investing purely in line with their overall tolerance towards risk and not in line with their physical capacity for loss. Another example would be an elderly client who is managing funds via a Trust for their family. Should they invest as cautiously as they would with their own money, also taking into account their potentially shorter-term horizon, or invest more adventurously over the longer term for the future generations?

Conversely, the same logic applies when it's time to start withdrawing money from investment accounts. Because the rules governing pension funds have become more liberal with regard to how much you can withdraw and when, it's important to be cautious. For example, you might not want to immediately withdraw money from a pension fund with adventurous investments until such time as the anticipated growth occurs, especially if you've matched that source of income to longer-term objectives. Instead, you might want to hold off on any withdrawals for five or ten years, and take the money from another account to pay current expenditures or to finance short-term goals.

Diversification: The "Free Lunch" of Investing

Many of the risks associated with investing can be controlled or even eliminated through the diversification of your investments. Although *some* risk will always remain, principally short-term volatility risk and/or inflation risk, most risk can be alleviated by employing a strategy of diversification.

What is diversification and how do you go about achieving it?

In its simplest form, diversification is adherence to the old adage of "not putting all your eggs in one basket." In other words, do not concentrate your investment strategy in too few opportunities. You can diversify an investment strategy in many ways:

Asset class: A mix of shares, bonds, cash, property, and other assets will be more suitable for most investors than a portfolio constructed from just one class.

Geography: Don't have your entire portfolio invested in U.K.-focused, Sterling-denominated assets. Investors all over the world have a "home bias," but there is no reason that this should be the case.

Market capitalisation: Don't have all your assets invested in larger companies. Smaller and medium-sized companies can offer returns that are just as good, if not better, while simultaneously spreading the risk.

Concentration: Your portfolio shouldn't be invested in a limited number of funds or companies. Most investment portfolios of any size should have around 10 funds within them. A portfolio of individual shares must contain at least 20 stocks to achieve a decent level of diversification. (Please note, though, that adding 10 additional funds to a 40-fund portfolio is unlikely to significantly improve diversification.)

The great benefit of diversification is that it can significantly reduce volatility while *not* systematically reducing returns. Modern Portfolio Theory, pioneered by Harry Markowitz in 1952, dictates that investors can reduce their portfolio volatility by incorporating investment opportunities with future returns that are not set to be perfectly correlated with each other. Ideally, you would include assets that are negatively correlated – that is, the value of one would probably increase at the same time that the other was declining.

Modern Portfolio Theory has also shown that it's possible to reduce portfolio volatility by incorporating assets that have a positive correlation, so long as the correlation is not perfect. In other words, both types of assets can rise (or fall) at the same time, but (provided they are not of the same magnitude), diversification can be achieved. In addition, the theory continues, you may be able to combine two assets together with identical expected returns (but different volatility expectations). As long as the assets' returns are not perfectly correlated, you may achieve the same overall return with any combination of the assets while potentially reducing volatility to a level below what you would see if you held just one of the assets. This is diversification in its simplest form. We simply extend the practice to hold numerous different investment opportunities.

The process of diversification has been at the centre of every well-constructed portfolio for the last 50 or so years. During this time, investors have been receiving something (reduced risk) for nothing (no expectation of reduced long-term returns). This is why diversification is known as "the one free lunch of investing."

Be Wary of Guarantees

In the English language, *guarantee* is a powerful word, and when it's attached to something positive, such as "capital security," it can be very alluring. Who wouldn't want a guarantee of capital security over their investment?

Given the natural pull towards guarantees, it can be difficult to dispassionately consider offers that are accompanied by guarantees. In my experience, however, three broad questions must be satisfactorily answered before committing funds to any product with a guarantee:

1. How secure is the guarantee? (Remember, a guarantee is only as strong as the person or persons providing it.)
2. What exactly is being guaranteed, and how important is this to you?
3. What is the cost of the guarantee, and by extension, what value is it meant to provide?

In our minds, once we have secured something that's guaranteed, it can never be taken away from us. In reality, though, this isn't always the case. Most financial guarantees are backed by an institution such as an investment bank. As we saw during the recent financial crisis, the value of such guarantees may not be worth the cost of the paper on which they're printed. Therefore, a direct and indirect impact must be noted.

For example, investors who had guarantees backed by Lehman Brothers were, in many cases, directly affected by the loss of the guarantee. Other investors were indirectly impacted by market concerns that other institutions could suffer the same fate as Lehman Brothers. Although the other institutions' guarantees may have remained in force, indirectly-impacted investors in, for example, structured products saw significant paper losses on their investments, even though their capital value was theoretically guaranteed.

When offered a guarantee, our first instinct is to accept it. However, we must always be careful about what the guarantee covers. Guarantees connected to investments usually cover either the capital value or the income derived from the investment. Therefore, each investor needs to ask, "How important is security of income or capital for this asset pot?

How would my standard of living be affected if the capital or income fell significantly?" If the answer in both cases is "not much," then do you really need such a guarantee?

Guarantees are useful in the right circumstances. For example, an individual who has capital available, but after a comprehensive budget planning analysis, determines that she needs substantial and ongoing income from her investment, would usually benefit greatly from a lifetime guarantee on income derived from the investment. The volatility of the capital is of limited concern when making sure that her income needs are met. However, if the income needed was not high and/or was likely to be of a short duration, then the risk of the capital being eroded, and hence the income ceasing, would be much reduced. In that case, the guaranteed income is of lesser value.

Finally, even when guaranteed income or capital is of value, always consider the cost of the guarantee. We now live in a world where returns are likely to be lower than those seen in decades past, even as market volatility remains high. The price offered for a guarantee, either explicitly as a direct charge or implicitly within the terms of a product, can easily eat into your after-tax returns. And, if the cost of the guarantee is high, this may offset some of the guarantee's value by limiting your returns.

The issue of guarantees lies at the heart of financial planning. It takes a skilled Financial Planner to properly understand a client's needs, financial and emotional, and appraise the suitability of an investment guarantee. In too many instances, expensive guarantees are sold to clients when, in reality, these guarantees were never really required.

The Need for Transparency

The financial landscape is awash with complex concepts, products, and solutions. Much of that complexity has actually been created by the financial services industry, often in an attempt to confuse others and give the impression of expertise. This complexity creates a lack of transparency for both investors and the public at large.

We use a strict method when considering new concepts or solutions. Although we, as financial services professionals, may understand the matters at hand, if we can't explain these concepts or product to our clients in a simple and straightforward manner, we don't employ these solutions. When considering a product on a client's behalf, we ask questions such as:

- Are the risks transparent? Every investment opportunity carries risk, and we need to understand the specific risks of the concept and how these may interact with a particular client. We are always reminding ourselves that if something appears to be too good to be true, then it usually is.
- Is the process or the return consistent and repeatable under different market conditions? Frequently, investment funds are promoted on the back of outstanding investment performance. This performance is usually measured over a relatively short timescale during which market conditions were particularly suited to the opportunity. Commercial property funds during the mid-2000s are a prime example. The question we ask is, "If things changed, what would be the impact upon this investment opportunity, and how would this product compare against other more proven opportunities?"
- Can it be easily understood? We have a combined experience of several decades in the financial services industry, but sometimes a concept is so complicated that it's difficult for us to understand all its features and risks. If an investment opportunity falls into that category, we discount it pretty quickly.
- Can we explain it easily? We may be able to understand the concept, but if we can't explain it clearly to a client for whom it would otherwise be suitable, we become concerned about proceeding. Naturally, this is dependent upon the knowledge and experience of the investor.

No Financial Planner has perfect foresight or knowledge. If you don't understand part of the investment process or product, then it is vital to ask questions or raise concerns. Any good Financial Planner should be happy to engage with you in such a dialogue.

Don't Underestimate the Need for Liquidity

A common trap into which many investors fall is being unable to access their funds at a time of real need. By its very nature, investing is a medium- to long-term venture. Therefore, there is no *inherent* problem with an investment that has (or might have) some sort of tie-in or restriction that prevents you from liquidating it immediately.

Here are some examples of when you might be locked into an investment:

Product-specific tie-ins: This clause to an investment means that funds cannot be withdrawn for a set period. The nature of the clause is dictated by the provider of the plan. Fortunately, such clauses are much less common than they once were.

Tax- or wrapper-specific restrictions: With this type of investment, a general restriction may apply during which exiting the investment is impossible or at least very costly. For example, investments made into pensions cannot be accessed in most cases until age 55. Enterprise Investment Schemes (EISs) will also claw-back the income tax rebate provided on the investment if a redemption is made during the first three years. Another example is being locked in to an investment for tax reasons as a result of previous gains. In other words, the tax payable upon the crystallised gains outweighs the benefits of any alternative.

Asset-specific issues: It's a fact of investing that certain assets take longer to sell. For example, shares in an FTSE 100-listed company can be sold almost instantly, whereas shares in private companies can take months, given the absence of a ready market for them. Anyone who has either bought or sold a house knows how long it can take from identifying a property and agreeing to a price to actually moving in.

Indivisibility: One common attraction of stock market investing is that investors can usually liquidate a small part of the portfolio relatively easily. However, more illiquid investments, particularly property, need to be sold in their entirety. Without resorting to costly financing, it's very difficult to sell one room of a house while retaining ownership of the balance.

Investors in assets that have one or more of the above features should acknowledge the liquidity risk. This is especially true when a degree of borrowing or other leverage is linked to the investment – for example, a buy-to-let mortgage on a residential property. Once investors acknowledge the potential liquidity issues, they must "stress test" against various scenarios in which they may need access. Do they have other funds to meet those requirements without having to access the potentially restricted investment?

Investments that incline toward illiquidity often form a large part of investors' portfolios, and there is no inherent problem with this as long as the investor is aware of the impact this may have on financial stability in a worst-case scenario. They must also ensure that a particular investment product is very likely to compensate for the liquidity risk by providing better returns than they'd probably realise from a more liquid investment.

The ultimate question is: How are your investments positioned in the event of an emergency? Could access to your investments be restricted and, if so, what would this mean to you?

Passive vs. Active Management

Another question to address upfront is whether to pursue a passive or an active investment management strategy. Put simply, a passive strategy focuses predominantly or exclusively on investing in funds that track a wider index, such as the FTSE 100 All-Share in the U.K. An active strategy involves one or more people actively and continually choosing investments for your fund, with a view to beating the market.

Historically, most actively managed investment portfolios do not succeed in beating the market, especially after costs are included. According to a recently published study, more than 50 percent of actively managed funds tracked over a five-year period failed to achieve the goal of outperforming the market.[10] If that doesn't sound too bad, consider that actively managed funds usually carry much higher costs, so many of these investors were not just getting lower returns than those who invested in passive funds, they also paid more for the "privilege." For these reasons, I believe passive investments should be the bedrock strategy of most portfolios.

In addition, because it's more difficult to outperform certain indexes, particularly in well-developed equity markets like those in the U.K. and the U.S., passive investments tend to work very well. (For bonds and emerging market investments, however, the passive investment track record isn't quite as good in equities and/or here in the U.K.)

Of course, it's important to put some thought into the indexes your passively managed funds track. Look at how widespread the indexes are that the investments try to follow. For example, a Russian equity tracker wouldn't be the most diversified investment, because it would be heavily weighted with natural resource companies, increasing its volatility. Funds tracking Russian equity indexes would better lend themselves to active management, as the manager could quickly move in and out of the investments as circumstances warranted.

A few of my clients enjoy picking and choosing particular shares in an effort to beat the markets, and I'm usually fine with that. In those cases, I tend to "quarantine" their actively managed investments from the rest of the portfolio, especially if playing the market is something of a hobby for them. I'll say, "If that's your pastime, feel free to pursue it. As long as any losses suffered won't impact your long-term goals, there's no problem. And if you make some money, so much the better."

Earlier in my career, I worked in reviewing and researching actively managed funds, so I've lived in both the active and passive management camps. Ultimately, I reached the conclusion that for most investors passive management is the way to go. The higher costs of actively managed investments don't make sense for many people, especially in a low-inflation, low-return environment. Today the difference in costs is 1 to 1.5 percent for many actively managed funds versus just 0.3 percent for passively managed funds. That's quite a difference in terms of returns. Always be aware of your investment costs to ensure that you receive sufficient value.

Costs

You should also calculate *indirect* costs when choosing investment products.

In addition to the direct fees paid for investment, consider how much money a particular investment will cost over the long term in unrealised returns. For example, let's say you choose a passive investment strategy instead of an active strategy, which saves you 1 percent in annual management fees. In addition to paying less in direct fees, you also earn more in compounded returns over the life of the investment. Why? Because money that would have otherwise been paid in management fees is now growing in the cheaper fund.

So if you have two identical investments that perform equally well, but one investment costs 1 percent less, the cheaper investment will produce more return. With the passage of time, that 1 percent extra will mushroom in value. Eventually, that original 1 percent in savings could produce 2 or 3 or 4 percent in additional earnings for you. For example, if you save 1 percent in fees per annum for 10 years with a particular fund, this will give you a total return on the investment that's 16.2 percent greater.

As an investor, you will always incur costs, and it's important to make sure that you'll get sufficient value for those costs before choosing the investment. At the very least, be aware that financial products do carry costs.

Fortunately, today's investment options tend to be much cheaper than those available five or ten years ago, particularly when it comes to pension plans. Today, we can find a good pension plan for you that will cost 0.5 percent a year for the administration *and* the funds, whereas five or six years ago, most people paid annual fees of 1 percent. These cost reductions are largely the result of changes in regulations and technology, which have lowered the costs of tracking and managing investments.

When (and When Not) to Review Investment Performance

Thanks to new technology and online platforms, it's easier than ever to monitor your investments' performance whenever you want. But just because you *can* track them regularly doesn't mean that you should.

Believe me, you don't want to be the kind of person who checks the value of his investments twice a day ... or probably even once a month. Obsessively monitoring the performance of your investments can encourage impatience for immediate results. At worst, it can promote a speculative mindset that undercuts the kind of medium- to long-term investment approach you should be cultivating. Because markets can be very volatile (it's not uncommon for a market to move up or down by a percentage point in a day), checking performance too often does little more than fuel mood swings ranging from exuberance to despair. The value of your investments can change quite a lot in a single week, but over time, they tend to look more consistent. I'd suggest that checking performance every six months to a year is fine, but don't check more often than that.

If you monitor performance more often, it becomes tempting to pour money into rising markets and then engage in panic selling when markets tumble. This is precisely the opposite of what a smart investor does. Always remember that smart investing is not some sort of game or respectable outlet for a gambling addiction. It's a means to an end – a way to finance personal goals and objectives by increasing the value of your current assets.

Avoid Speculation

Over the long run, the people who profit most from stock market investing are contrarians – those who do the opposite of what everyone else is doing. What "everyone else is doing" is best summarised by the Four-Phase "Cycle of Emotions in Trading."

1. *Optimism.* When markets are surging, people who normally don't invest become captivated by the idea of getting rich overnight. "Expert" market analysts crawl out of the woodwork to pronounce that this is the time for the average person to enter the game because the forecast is rosy for the foreseeable future, and/or this particular market is unlike any other (in that it will never crash). Optimism and exuberance become contagious to the point where everyone seems to be offering advice, analysis, and day-by-day market updates.
2. *Euphoria.* As the market peaks, and everyone is earning money no matter which investment products they chose, so does (almost) everyone's sense of euphoria. The mantra is "Everything is gaining value and always will." Existing investors plough more money into the markets while new investors are eager to join the party.

3. *Fear.* Inevitably, the markets do decline, sparking fear among the masses. Adding fuel to the fire is the sudden appearance of a "new" set of market commentators stating that stock prices are now inflated and a "market correction" is overdue. (To be fair, there are always a few contrarian analysts who warn everyone, in advance, to avoid getting carried away by euphoria, but the average investor usually ignores the "Cassandras" until the predictions come true, by which time it's too late.)
4. *Panic.* As the market continues its slide and eventually bottoms out, many novice investors (those who have never seen such low prices) sell their stocks as if they were infected with the plague. The optimistic experts are either silent or long gone, leaving the small investors bereft of sage advice. What most of them do next is follow the crowd by selling, selling, selling! Later, most of the small investors return to their pre-market lives determined to never again put their money in risky investments.

That's what everyone else does.

By contrast, the contrarian is not trying to get rich quick. The contrarian realises that if she can earn modest returns every year, while enjoying compound interest, she'll do just fine over the long run. She is also not trying to find the best possible investments, but trying to avoid bad investments and bad strategies. By doing this, she'll probably outperform most other investors.

Contrarianism

Like everyone else, the contrarian wants to buy low and sell high. The main differences between the contrarian and everyone else are:

1. The contrarian actually *heeds* that advice; and
2. Once the contrarian succeeds in buying low – often during market downturns when everyone else is selling – she sits back and waits for prices to rise over the long term, rather than

trying to time the market in a futile effort to pick investments that will outperform the indexes over the short term.

The contrarian is not a short-term thinker or a compulsive gambler. She keeps her eyes on the prize, not the daily performance of her investments. Yes, we've all heard stories about people who invested in this or that "hot stock" and become millionaires – as well as the interior decorator at Facebook – but those aren't realistic expectations. Some people play the lottery and win, but that doesn't mean *you* should play today.

As a contrarian investor, I get scared when the market goes up a lot, and excited when it goes down, and I try to pass this attitude to my clients. The best opportunities abound when the market is low.

Some of the most fabled investment managers such as Warren Buffett, as well as famous U.K. fund managers including Neil Woodford and Anthony Bolton, have been contrarians. They made their money (and in one case nearly got fired during the technology rush of the 1990s for being bearish on technology stocks) and made their reputations by being contrarians. By doing this, they've succeeded in turning a famous aphorism by economist John Maynard Keynes on its head: "The market can remain irrational longer than you can remain solvent."

On paper, it may seem easy to become a contrarian, but especially during bull markets, it can be downright painful. While everyone else is enjoying fast and easy profits, you'll be chugging along with comparatively modest returns, and nobody will want to listen to your bearish sentiments. You'll be the odd man out, the cynic, the sceptic … until things once again "go south," at which point you'll be hailed as a farsighted genius … until the markets rise again and the process repeats itself.

To help you pass the lonely days and nights, feel free to adopt this quote as your own. It's from the American satirist and curmudgeon H.L. Mencken: "No one ever went broke underestimating the intelligence of the American public."

Prepare for Disappointment

There is no investment that won't perform poorly at various times, so prepare to be disappointed some of the time. It's *going* to happen, which is why we tell clients, "We're coming over to meet with you once a year. At two or three of those meetings over the next 10 years, we'll have very good news to report, and at another two or three meetings, we'll have really bad news for you. At other meetings, the news will be okay, but probably not spectacular." The subtext of these messages is, "Even if we do our jobs properly, you should expect that on average, two or three years out of ten will be bad."

You're going to be disappointed at times. It's going to cause you concern, especially if we run your cash-flow analysis and determine that some of the things you thought you could afford in the coming year are temporarily beyond your reach. It's just one of those things. As much as we'd like to, we can't control what the market's going to do. For this reason, we advise clients not to *depend* on receiving every last penny forecast by a best-case scenario. Never put yourself in the position of relying on money that may not materialise when you want it or need it.

It's also important to note that the range of projected outcomes becomes narrower as you get older. We have much more confidence saying to someone in their eighties, "Look, you've got this income, you've got these assets, including your house. There is less uncertainty, once you have achieved financial independence and are in later life, care fees aside. Your lifestyle is set, you don't have the other potential costs and expenses that younger people have."

Exploit Time, Not Timing

What does this mean, "exploit time, not timing?" Basically, it means that the longer you're invested in the market, the better. What matters is not so much when you enter or exit the market – the *timing* of coming in and going out – but the *length* of time you stay in the market.

Given how quickly markets react, it's very difficult to know when it's best to enter or leave. By the time you *think* you've identified the right time, your information is probably out of date. And according to a recent analysis, those who try to time their entry and exit may miss important "bounces."[11]

For example, an investor in global stocks who remained in the markets from 31 December 2002 to 31 December 2012 would have enjoyed a cumulative return of 68.96 percent. However, by missing the market's 10 best days, he would have lost 4.64 percent of his assets. Missing the market's 20 best days would have cost the same investor 32.19 percent of his assets, while missing the best 30 days would have left him in the hole by 49.08 percent.[12]

The same analysis also revealed that by staying invested in global stocks for periods of 12 years or more between 1980 and 2012, an investor would have reduced his chances of seeing a negative return to zero.[13] That's right. Zero.

The bottom line is that discipline breeds success over the long term. The longer you stay invested, the greater the likelihood that your investments will generate positive returns. So don't worry about what the market's doing on any one day or one week. In tandem with your Financial Planner, formulate a plan to drip in your money, and once your investment strategy is established, don't deviate from the plan.

Rebalancing

Over time, different asset classes produce different returns. Consequently, if you establish a Strategic Asset Allocation of 50 percent equities and 50 percent bonds, and then do nothing, the equities will eventually outperform the bonds, causing equities to represent a larger share of the total pie. And because equities are more volatile than bonds, allowing the portfolio to become unbalanced will increase your risk. Rebalancing the portfolio will restore the original 50/50 split.

Hence, the main goal of rebalancing is to minimise risk rather than maximise returns.

In theory, you and your Financial Planner will select a rebalancing strategy that weighs your willingness to accept risk against expected returns.

Rebalancing is typically automated these days. However, reallocations can also be done manually following reviews of a Strategic

Asset Allocation or Tactical Asset Allocation policy, though the latter carries significant risks as well as potential rewards. Keep in mind that the more "rebalancing events" you undertake every year, the higher your costs in terms of time and fees.

How often should you rebalance your portfolio? It's advisable to rebalance at least once a year, and as often as every six months or every quarter. You're unlikely to obtain a meaningful increase in returns by rebalancing more often, but you may see a meaningful increase in costs.

Rebalancing doesn't always add value, particularly in the short term, because rebalancing effectively forces you to buy low and sell high. This means you're continually selling investments that have risen in value and buying those that have declined, so in rampant bull markets, rebalancing tends to dampen performance. On the positive side, rebalancing protects you during bear markets.

Ultimately, rebalancing is a cornerstone of any sensible investment strategy.

Don't Let the "Tax Tail" Wag the "Investment Dog"

Some investments exist solely for their tax benefits. This doesn't mean you shouldn't select them, but you need to understand that, as a result of the tax benefits, your returns might be anaemic. The tax benefits might outweigh that disadvantage, but in most cases they don't.

At the moment, for example, the government is encouraging people to invest in smaller start-up companies. To do this, they are offering attractive tax benefits (tax breaks) on these investments. Venture Capital Trusts (VCTs) and Enterprise Investment Schemes (EISs) are just two examples of this. Depending upon your tax position, you can save quite a lot of tax by investing in such schemes. In some cases, people have received up to 70 percent of the value of the investment as tax relief in one form or another. In those instances, even if the investments declined by 70 percent, they didn't lose money.

As a rule, however, it pays to be careful. Investing in something for the purpose of earning 10 percent or 20 percent in tax benefits is not a clever plan. Always scrutinise the investment. Ask yourself, "Does this fit with my overall investment strategy?" Only if the answer is "yes" should you then inquire about tax benefits – as opposed to reversing the process: "Are there any tax benefits? Yes? Then let's put some money there."

The standard procedure for smart investors is to *first* ask, "What's the right investment strategy for me?" The lesser priority is "How can I invest tax-efficiently, given the various wrappers available?"

If you're a particularly high earner, paying a lot of income tax, it might make sense to divert some of your money into more complex and risky investments, despite any lock-in and tie-in periods. Alternatively, some providers offer lower-risk versions of these schemes, which might be appropriate for people who aren't that wealthy. Regardless, you must always determine the most appropriate mix of assets in which to invest before focusing on any tax benefits. In short, don't let the "tax tail" wag the "investment dog."

Create a Written Investment Policy Mandate

Creating a written record of your investment policy offers you a number of advantages. First, the process of creating the document ensures that all considerations are appraised prior to implementing the strategy, reducing the likelihood of any errors of omission. Second, when a strategy is reviewed, you have a ready-made reference point by which performance can be measured. Third, an investment mandate helps you commit to the strategy. For example, if during a performance review you note that one aspect of a strategy has performed particularly well, it might be tempting to add further to such positions, increasing your dependency on a particular asset or fund. But this approach is usually flawed. The best-performing sector of yesterday is often tomorrow's laggard. Having a written document that confirms the allocation to a particular opportunity – and which describes how exposure to this investment type can be varied – will help thwart this temptation. This technique also works to prevent investors from cutting poor-performing but valuable assets or funds from the strategic mix.

The investment mandate commonly features some or all of the following:

- The names of the owners of the strategy.
- The assets covered by the mandate, and how these relate to all (or part) of the total investable funds.
- A description of the overall objective of the strategy (retirement, education funding, etc.).
- An overall timescale for the strategy.
- The requirement for growth and/or income. (For the latter, the income amount and frequency should be specified.)
- A proposed long-term strategic asset allocation for the portfolio (cash, bonds, commercial property, and U.K. and overseas equities are usually the main asset classes).
- The benchmark indices that will be used to measure performance (e.g., the FTSE All Share index for the portfolio's U.K. equity component).
- A guide to the maximum expected drawdown (or loss) of the portfolio. This is particularly important if the portfolio is being managed by an outsourced investment professional, such as a Discretionary Fund Manager (DFM).
- A long-term asset-allocation tolerance around which any asset exposure is allowed to vary. (+/- 10 percent is a common tolerance.) So, for example, a long-term exposure to U.K. Equities of 25 percent can comfortably vary between 15 percent and 35 percent, depending upon market conditions. Confirmation also needs to be provided of how long it would be permissible, if at all, for the portfolio to remain outside these boundaries.
- The amount of leeway given to include other assets within the strategy – those that aren't covered within the long-term strategic asset allocation.
- A cap on exposure to any single share, bond or fund (10 percent of the total usually makes sense).
- A note on how often rebalancing and formal reviews should occur. At a minimum, both should take place annually.

- A note on the liquidity of the portfolio and any limits on including positions that could not be liquidated within a certain time.
- Applicable comments concerning tax strategy. For instance, a portfolio that includes funds held both inside and outside of the ISA shelter may suggest that certain types of assets should be held within the ISA component and vice-versa.
- Confirmation of the term over which performance is to be measured. A rolling three-year basis is standard.
- Any specific items that need to be considered within the portfolio, such as ethical considerations or requirements to hold specific assets in the portfolio.

I encourage all investors to create their own mandates. If you are being advised by a Financial Planner, ask them to provide you with one.

The Voice of Reason

I believe that every sensible Financial Planner should act as a contrarian, as a voice of reason. I often feel most comfortable doing the opposite of what everyone else thinks. When the conventional wisdom dictates that now is the "best" time to invest, I tend to worry. By the same token, when others suggest that the bottom has fallen out of the markets, I search for opportunities. In my opinion, Financial Planners have three primary responsibilities when it comes to setting investment strategies:

1. To help clients align their strategies with their personal and financial goals.
2. To help clients reach their destinations safely and with a minimum of discomfort.
3. To prevent, as best they can, their clients from making foolish decisions.

All three responsibilities are best fulfilled from the very beginning of the planning process – during early discussions about establishing realistic goals, setting realistic expectations, and assessing their physical, emotional, and experiential risk.

6A. Clarity Developer

UNDERSTANDING WHAT IS IMPORTANT TO YOU

Having a deep understanding of your priorities and issues is central to the art of financial planning. We will discuss such matters together but these pages can start the process of developing such an appreciation of yourself and your future goals.

Please take time to consider the questions proffered below before recording your responses.

If you feel the need to discuss these questions with us before we formally review your responses, please do not hesitate to get in touch.

Question One – The R-Factor Question®
If we were meeting three years from today and we were looking back over those three years, what would have to have happened during that period for you to feel happy with your progress?

Question Two
Considering the responses given above, if you were able to achieve only three of your aims, which (in order of priority) would they be?

Question Three – D.O.S.®
Looking again at your responses to question one, what would be the greatest dangers that could stop you from achieving your aims?

What would be the biggest opportunities within your aims that should be captured?

And what are the greatest current strengths you have that you'll need to build upon to help you achieve your aims?

Remember this is only a snapshot in time, reflecting where you are today. How you rate your intentions could change at a later date.

Understanding Your Philosophy Towards Investments

An appreciation of your future aims and objectives needs to be considered alongside your comfort and understanding towards investing. One for instance cannot quantify one's ability to meet one's objectives without first developing a rational expectation of what, if any, return could be achieved upon the investments required to fund the objective.

The following questions will help you start the process of developing a deeper understanding of what you do, and perhaps more importantly, what you do not feel comfortable with regarding investing your capital towards meeting your goals.

Question Four:
In the event that your investments were ahead of expectations, which of the following would you be most prepared to decrease?
- ☐ The risk of your investments.
- ☐ The timescale until your objectives are realised.
- ☐ The amount you are investing.
- ☐ None of the above.

Question Five:
In the event that your investments were behind expectations, which of the following would you be most prepared to increase?
- ☐ The risk of your investments.
- ☐ The timescale until your objectives are realised.
- ☐ The amount you are investing.
- ☐ None of the above.

Question Six:
Assuming a ten-year investment horizon, if your investment portfolio was to underperform against expectations for both the first and second year of investment, would you:
- ☐ Accept that this was a short-term fluctuation in long-term returns.

- ☐ Seek a higher level of return accepting that this would increase the risks taken within your investments.
- ☐ Accept the lower return achieved because you do not want a higher level of risk but accepting that your goals may take longer to achieve.
- ☐ Look to inject more capital into the portfolio.

Question Seven:
How familiar are you with investment matters?
- ☐ Very limited knowledge.
- ☐ Moderate knowledge.
- ☐ Reasonably extensive knowledge.
- ☐ I am an expert.

Question Eight:
What is your main aim when considering an investment?
- ☐ Protecting the capital value, even if it means low total returns.
- ☐ Beating inflation by a moderate margin.
- ☐ A high total return and not too concerned about short-term capital loss.
- ☐ A very high total return with limited regard for short-term capital loss.

Question Nine:
If the value of your investments were to drop by 20% in the space of a few months, which of the following would best describe your reaction? Would you:
- ☐ Sell most of the assets to limit further losses.
- ☐ Start to have sleepless nights.
- ☐ Do nothing, knowing that markets can fall and hoping for a reversal in due course.
- ☐ Invest more money into the depressed markets where there are suitable opportunities.

Question Ten:

One important aspect of investing is to at least maintain an investment's real value compared with the cost of living (inflation). Do you expect the annual returns from your investments to:
- ☐ Beat inflation by up to 2%.
- ☐ Beat inflation by between 2% and 4%.
- ☐ Beat inflation by between 4% and 6%.
- ☐ Beat inflation by more than 6%.

Question Eleven:

It is suggested to you by a friend that high returns can be achieved by borrowing money and investing in a "speculative" investment. A speculative investment tends to offer the potential for a high return but at the cost of taking more risk. Would you:
- ☐ Follow the advice without hesitation.
- ☐ Be tempted but would seek professional advice.
- ☐ Totally dismiss as far too risky.

Question Twelve:

Do you consider your attitude to financial risk to be:
- ☐ Very much more speculative than average.
- ☐ Quite adventurous.
- ☐ Above average.
- ☐ More risk averse.

Question Thirteen:

If you were offered a potential investment opportunity that was described as "a bit risky but could have great potential," what would your first thoughts be?
- ☐ This could be a dangerous thing to do.
- ☐ The returns will be uncertain.
- ☐ This could be an opportunity to achieve high returns.

The full set of questions and more details are available online:
thefamilylegacysolution.co.uk

7. Progress Appraisals

TO ENSURE THAT YOU STAY ON TRACK – that you are saving enough, generating healthy returns on your investments, and maintaining sufficient cash flow – the financial plan must be regularly reviewed and (if necessary) adjusted. In almost every case, this should be done at least once a year, and even more often when your circumstances change or a major life event occurs.

The Door Should Always Be Open

At The Family Legacy Solution, we meet with clients annually to catch up with them and review their plans, but we also maintain contact throughout the year via phone calls and correspondence – if only to remind them that we're here to answer any questions or concerns. As a financial planning client, you should always feel that your planner's door is open. Keep in mind that planners are not primarily salespeople who limit themselves to providing one-time services or once-a-year checkups. They should also be available to offer advice and recommendations about a wide range of issues. Good planners don't charge by the hour for these ongoing services, so if you have a problem or want a second opinion, don't be shy about asking.

If absolutely nothing has happened since the plan was implemented, or since the previous review, there may be little to discuss. However, any change of circumstances or imminent change warrants a discussion. When it comes to planning, I dislike surprises. I prefer to learn about changes *before* they happen. One of the worst things a planner can encounter is learning about a major life event or change in circumstances after the fact – when it may be too late to make adjustments or change directions. No matter how small or insignificant an event might seem, it is better to be safe than sorry. Inform your Financial Planner about it as soon as you're able – particularly if one of your appointed executors or trustees is taken ill or dies.

Note: Once upon a time, review meetings sometimes involved "rebalancing" of the portfolios, but today this is normally done automatically throughout the year. In fact, manual rebalancing is a very rare occurrence. And make no mistake: rebalancing and reviews are not interchangeable terms. Rebalancing involves periodically buying or selling assets in the portfolio to maintain your desired level of asset allocation. For example, if your original target asset allocation was 50 percent stocks and 50 percent bonds, but the value of the stocks has since risen to the point where they now comprise 60 percent of your portfolio's value, rebalancing ensures that you return to the desired 50/50 level of asset allocation. A review is a different animal. Its purpose is to make sure that the plan is performing according to your expectations and is being properly implemented. Here the key tool at our disposal is the cash-flow analysis, which normally tells us whether everything is going smoothly or if course corrections should be considered.

Focus on Ends, Not Just Means

Investment reviews are an important component of review meetings, but should not be over-emphasised, as this can sometimes cause people to get bogged down in minutiae. Achieving your goals is the ultimate aim of the planning process, not obsessing over the means by which those goals are to be realised.

Some people place too much emphasis on investment performance, which is akin to focusing on a few trees rather than the forest. In my view, once investments have been set up, it's best to leave them alone for six to twelve months. Just forget about them. Don't check online. Don't assess your investment performance every day or every week. Don't worry about them. Obsessing over performance leads to trouble. One of the most important responsibilities of a Financial Planner is protecting clients from themselves, and toward this end, contrarian thinking is a very important trait. Performance-obsessed clients usually want to invest more when everything looks rosy. Money always flows to stock investments when markets rise, and then dries up when the markets fall. My job is to prevent this behaviour, or better still, to reverse it. When the news is bad, your planner should try to sell you on the notion of establishing new positions. When the prevailing mood is dark, he should help you see the value of buying low. Influencing behaviour to align it with your own best interests is a hallmark of a good Financial Planner.

I'm not suggesting that performance analyses have no place during reviews – only that you shouldn't place so much focus on them while ignoring the overall financial plan. If you spend too much time trying to determine why an investment is returning 4 percent when you'd hoped for 5 percent, this can steal time and focus away from much more important matters.

For example, while conducting the cash-flow analysis for a recent retiree, I projected a 5 percent long-term average return, in accordance with my understanding of the client's risk tolerance. Thereafter, he became unduly fixated on that figure of 5 percent. Although I had established other composite benchmarks for the investments, and his returns were broadly in line with those benchmarks, the investments grew by 4 percent rather than 5 percent during the first two years. Unfortunately, the client was so obsessed with that 5 percent return that he ignored the fact that all of his key financial aims were either met or exceeded.

Always stay focused on the big picture. Always stay focused on your key goals. The true measure of a financial plan is not whether this or that investment product returns a specific percentage within six or twelve months, but whether the overall plan helps you realise the benefits of financial independence.

Appendix

ALTHOUGH MOST OF MY CLIENTS at The Family Legacy Solution are nearing retirement or are already retired, there is no bad time to plan for a more secure financial future and to ensure that loved ones are protected against "what if" disasters. And there is *definitely* no bad time to start saving and investing surplus income so that financial independence is someday within reach. Sadly, many people in their twenties and thirties give little or no thought to long-term financial planning and "what if" contingencies. At a minimum, the sooner you begin saving and investing, the sooner you'll start accumulating and growing the assets you need to achieve financial independence – something that need not (and should not) be postponed until "retirement age."

With this in mind, below are four financial-planning and legacy-planning concerns that younger adults should address as soon as possible.

Budget Planning

In this area, my recommendations to younger people are mostly the same as those to older clients. Create a budget using a system that divides expenses into three distinct types.

Core (bills that are likely to continue indefinitely) – it's vital to consider all of your regular monthly expenditure items. Most people start by listing what I call "core" expenditures, those they see coming out of their bank account every month. Some examples include:
- ☐ Rent.
- ☐ Food, drink, and household products.
- ☐ Building and contents insurance premiums.
- ☐ Utility bills.
- ☐ Travel expenses including car fuel.
- ☐ Car depreciation.

- White goods.
- Property maintenance.

Financial (expenditures relating to a specific financial asset such as a mortgage or insurance premiums).

Discretionary: (all other expenditures – mainly those that could be forsaken if circumstances dictate). Examples include holidays and gifts.

Creating a budget allows you to make more informed decisions. When preparing a budget for the first time, many people are surprised at how much they are spending in certain categories, especially on discretionary expenditures.

The Six Jars Philosophy

In my experience, the most common reason that people don't save enough is that they have no strategy for how to allocate surplus income for short-term, medium-term, and long-term needs and goals. To remedy this, I recommend that you adopt the income-allocation technique known as the "Six Jars," a money management technique that focuses on building wealth. With this system, you place set percentages of your after-tax income into six jars (or accounts) in the following amounts:

- **Necessities (55 percent):** The income placed in this jar is for your everyday expenditures such as fuel, rent, and utilities.
- **Financial Independence (10 percent):** The money put into this jar is for investments and savings. You shouldn't touch this money until you achieve financial independence – and even then, it's best to spend only the returns on investments, not the principal.
- **Debt-Reduction (10 percent):** This is money you devote to paying down mortgages and other consumer loans. In the absence of debt, it can also be used as a "rainy day fund." Note: This money is *in addition* to sums used for normal repayments.
- **Long-Term Savings (10 percent):** This is money that can be used to finance big-ticket purchases such as a home, car, or

your children's education. In other words, it's for known longer-term expenditures.
- ☐ **Play (10 percent):** As the label indicates, these funds are devoted to leisure and enjoyment. Go on holiday, take a date to an expensive restaurant, or enjoy a night on the town. Whatever you decide, make it special. As a rule, you should accumulate this money for no longer than three months before spending it.
- ☐ **Charity (5 percent):** This money is for giving to others, including charitable donations.

There are different rules of thumb on the exact percentages to allocate to each jar or account, but we typically tell people that they shouldn't allocate more than 55 percent of their take-home income to the Necessities Jar. In other words, we advise clients to target no more than 55 percent of their total after-tax income for funding their current lifestyles.

By the way, these rules apply to *income*. For lump sums you receive such as gifts, bonuses, or inheritances, we recommend that nothing go into the Necessities Jar and 50 percent into the Financial Independence Jar. Long-Term Savings should receive 15 percent, Play 10 percent, Charity 5 percent, and Debt Reduction 20 percent.

Insurance

Young people tend to be massively underinsured. True, you don't really need life insurance if you have no dependents – if you're single, have no children, and don't have a mortgage. However, keep in mind that your biggest asset is your ability to earn, so if you're ever unable to work for any reason, you could find yourself in big trouble if you aren't insured.

In the event of long-term illness or disability, you don't want to rely upon state or employer benefits. The benefits are too limited and/or temporary. This is another reason to engage in some budget planning. You'll want to perform "what if" analyses to determine how much income you'd need in the event you couldn't work for an extended period. Ask yourself this hypothetical question, "If I weren't working, what still needs to be paid – my core and financial expenditures?"

Make sure you are protected by an insurance policy, preferably a permanent health insurance policy, which is one that pays out until either you get better or reach the end of the term (normally retirement age) or you die. These policies are medically underwritten at the outset, so they don't automatically exclude pre-existing conditions. They tend to be more expensive than the alternatives, but they provide a much better value in terms of benefits.

If you *do* have a spouse/partner or dependents, consider a life insurance policy that will provide them with a lump sum in the event of your death. To determine how much will be needed requires (again) some budget planning. Start by totalling all of the household debts, and then add to that figure the lump-sum of capital that would be needed to eliminate any income shortfalls. Use a figure somewhere between 3 percent and 5 percent as a capitalised figure. For example, if you wanted your spouse to receive £20,000 per annum, you would need to allot at least 20 times that sum as your capital amount (£400,000). On top of that, you might want to add still more capital to help put your children through university or other goals.

Essentially, there are three types of expenses for which you need insurance: debt, income shortfalls, and future one-offs. Analysing these needs will give you a rough idea of the amount of insurance you'll need in the event of your death.

Wills and Lasting Power of Attorney

Even if you draft an extremely simple Will, it's better than taking a chance on dying intestate. (*See the section on Wills in Chapter 4.*)

It's also important to prepare a Lasting Power of Attorney in the event you become unable to make your own decisions. There are two types of Lasting Power of Attorney: (1) health and welfare and (2) property and financial affairs. You can choose to make one type or both, provided you're over 18 years of age and have the ability to make your own decisions at the time the document is executed.

A health and welfare Lasting Power of Attorney allows you to choose at least one person to make decisions that impact your daily routines, medical care, and life-sustaining treatments. This type of Lasting Power of Attorney can be used only when you're unable to make your own decisions.

A property and financial affairs Power of Attorney lets you choose one person or more to make decisions about money and property on your behalf – paying bills, collecting benefits, selling your home. This type of Lasting Power of Attorney can be implemented as soon as it's registered.[14]

Young people tend to think that they won't die or become seriously ill or incapacitated, but it happens all the time. It's good to hope for the best – or even avoid thinking about such issues – as long as you prepare for the worst.

---

1 Graeme Paton, 'Cost of a degree to rise to £26,000 after tuition fee hike.' The Telegraph, 11 July, 2013
2 'Deprivation of assets in the means test for care home provision.' Factsheet 40, April 2014. www.ageuk.org.uk
3 'Should will writing be a reserved legal activity?' presentation to LSB will-writing workshop, Office of Fair Trading, 2010
4 'Cowboy Will Writing: Incompetence and dishonesty in the UK wills market', STEP Policy Briefing, January 2011
5 http://www.worcestergroup.com.au/page/34/Wills.html
6 http://www.adviceguide.org.uk/england/relationships_e/relationships_death_and_wills_e/wills.htm
7 https://www.gov.uk/inheritance-tax/gifts-and-exemptions
8 http://www.rjssolicitors.com/latest-news/2018-an-inheritance-tax-time-bomb
9 'A primer on tactical asset allocation strategic evaluation.' Vanguard Research, July 2010
10 'Enhanced practice management: The case for combining active and passive strategies in the UK.' Vanguard Research, September 2014
11 'Time in the market, not timing the market.' Fidelity Worldwide Investment, January 2013
12 Ibid.
13 'Time in the market, not timing the market.' Fidelity Worldwide Investment, January 2013
14 https://www.gov.uk/power-of-attorney/overview

Made in the USA
Charleston, SC
20 April 2015